Wickham Hoffman

Camp, Court and Siege

A Narrative of personal Adventure and Observation during two Wars: 1861-1865;

1870-1871

Wickham Hoffman

Camp, Court and Siege
A Narrative of personal Adventure and Observation during two Wars: 1861-1865; 1870-1871

ISBN/EAN: 9783337176433

Printed in Europe, USA, Canada, Australia, Japan

Cover: Foto ©ninafisch / pixelio.de

More available books at **www.hansebooks.com**

CAMP COURT AND SIEGE

A NARRATIVE OF PERSONAL ADVENTURE AND
OBSERVATION DURING TWO WARS

1861–1865   1870–1871

By WICKHAM HOFFMAN

ASSISTANT ADJ.-GEN. U. S. VOLS. AND SECRETARY U. S. LEGATION AT PARIS

LONDON
SAMPSON LOW, MARSTON, SEARLE, & RIVINGTON
CROWN BUILDINGS, 188 FLEET STREET.
1877

Dedication.

TO

The Hon. E. B. WASHBURNE,

MINISTER OF THE U. S. AT PARIS,
THESE PAGES ARE CORDIALLY DEDICATED,
IN ADMIRATION OF THE STERLING QUALITIES OF MANHOOD
DISPLAYED BY HIM DURING THE DARK DAYS OF THE SIEGE
AND COMMUNE, AND IN RECOLLECTION OF MANY
PLEASANT HOURS PASSED TOGETHER DURING
AN OFFICIAL CONNECTION OF
NEARLY SIX YEARS.

CONTENTS.

CHAPTER I.

Hatteras.—"Black Drink."—Fortress Monroe.—General Butler.—Small-pox.—"L'Isle des Chats."—Lightning.—Farragut.—Troops land.—Surrender of Forts.................... Page 11

CHAPTER II.

New Orleans.—Custom-house.—Union Prisoners.—The Calaboose.—"Them Lincolnites."—The St. Charles.—"Grape-vine Telegraph."—New Orleans Shop-keepers.—Butler and Soulé.—The Fourth Wisconsin.—A New Orleans Mob.—Yellow Fever.......... 23

CHAPTER III.

Vicksburg.—River on Fire.—Baton Rouge.—Start again for Vicksburg.—The *Hartford*.—The Canal.—Farragut.—Captain Craven.—The *Arkansas*.—Major Boardman.—The *Arkansas* runs the Gauntlet.—Malaria.................................. 35

CHAPTER IV.

Sickness.—Battle of Baton Rouge.—Death of Williams.—"Fix Bayonets!"—Thomas Williams.—His Body.—General T. W. Sherman.—Butler relieved.—General Orders, No. 10.—Mr. Adams and Lord Palmerston.—Butler's Style................... 47

CHAPTER V.

T. W. Sherman.—Contrabands.—Defenses of New Orleans.—Exchange of Prisoners.—Amenities in War.—Port Hudson.—Reconnoissance in Force.—The Fleet.—Our Left.—Assault of May 27th.—Sherman wounded.—Port Hudson surrenders.......... Page 59

CHAPTER VI.

Major-general Franklin.—Sabine Pass.—Collision at Sea.—March through Louisiana.—Rebel Correspondence.—"The Gypsy's Wassail."—Rebel Women.—Rebel Poetry.—A Skirmish.—Salt Island.—Winter Climate.—Banks's Capua.—Major Joseph Bailey..... 74

CHAPTER VII.

Mistakes.—Affair at Mansfield.—Peach Hill.—Freaks of the Imagination.—After Peach Hill.—General William Dwight.—Retreat to Pleasant Hill.—Pleasant Hill.—General Dick Taylor.—Taylor and the King of Denmark.—An Incident...................... 87

CHAPTER VIII.

Low Water.—The Fleet in Danger.—We fall back upon Alexandria.—Things look Gloomy.—Bailey builds a Dam in ten Days.—Saves the Fleet.—A Skirmish.—Smith defeats Polignac.—Unpopularity of Foreign Officers.—A Novel Bridge.—Leave of Absence.—A Year in Virginia.—Am ordered again to New Orleans......... 98

CHAPTER IX.

Visit to Grant's Head-quarters.—His Anecdotes of Army Life.—Banks relieved.—Canby in Command.—Bailey at Mobile.—Death of Bailey.—Canby as a Civil Governor.—Confiscated Property.—Proposes to rebuild Levees.—Is stopped by Sheridan.—Canby appeals.

—Is sustained, but too late.—Levees destroyed by Floods.—Conflict of Jurisdiction.—Action of President Johnson.—Sheridan abolishes Canby's Provost Marshal's Department.—Canby asks to be recalled.—Is ordered to Washington.—To Galveston.—To Richmond.—To Charleston.—Is murdered by the Modocs.—His Character. Page 105

CHAPTER X.

The Writer appointed Assistant Secretary of Legation to Paris.—Presented to the Emperor.—Court Balls.—Diplomatic Dress.—Opening of Corps Législatif.—Opening of Parliament.—King of the Belgians.—Emperor of Austria.—King of Prussia.—Queen Augusta.—Emperor Alexander.—Attempt to assassinate him.—Ball at Russian Embassy.—Resignation of General Dix 119

CHAPTER XI.

Washburne appointed Minister.—Declaration of War.—Thiers opposes it.—The United States asked to protect Germans in France.—Fish's Instructions.—Assent of French Government given.—Paris in War-paint.—The Emperor opposed to War.—Not a Free Agent.—His *Entourage.*—Marshal Le Bœuf 134

CHAPTER XII.

Germans forbidden to leave Paris.—Afterward expelled.—Large Number in Paris.—Americans in Europe.—Emperor's Staff an Incumbrance.—French Generals.—Their Rivalries.—False News from the Front.—Effect in Paris.—Reaction.—Expulsion of Germans.—Sad Scenes.—Washburne's Action.—Diplomatic Service.—Battle of Sedan.—Sheridan at Sedan 145

CHAPTER XIII.

Revolution of September 4th, 1870.—Paris *en Fête.*—Flight of the Empress.—Saved by Foreigners.—Escapes in an English Yacht.—

Government of National Defense.—Trochu at its Head.—Jules Simon.—United States recognizes Republic.—Washburne's Address.—Favre's Answer.—Efforts for Peace.—John L. O'Sullivan. Page 159

CHAPTER XIV.

Belleville Demonstrates.—Radical Clubs.—Their Blasphemy and Violence.—Unreasonable Suspicion.—Outrages.—Diplomatic Corps.—Some of them leave Paris.—Meeting of the Corps.—Votes not to Leave.—Embassadors and Ministers.—Right of Correspondence in a Besieged Place.—Commencement of Siege, September 19th.—Besiegers and Besieged.—Advantages of Besieged............ 170

CHAPTER XV.

Balloons.—Large Number dispatched.—Small Number lost.—Worth. —Carrier-pigeons.—Their Failure.—Their Instincts.—*Times* "Agony Column."—Correspondence.—Letters to Besieged.—Count Solms.—Our Dispatch-bag.—Moltke complains that it is abused.—Washburne's Answer.—Bismarck's Reply................. 182

CHAPTER XVI.

Burnside's Peace Mission.—Sent in by Bismarck.—Interview with Trochu.—The Sympathetic Tear.—Question of Revictualment.—Failure of Negotiations.—Point of Vanity.—Flags of Truce.—French accused of Violation of Parole.—Question of the Francs-Tireurs.—Foreigners refused Permission to leave Paris.—Washburne insists.—Permission granted.—Departure of Americans.—Scenes at Creteil 196

CHAPTER XVII.

Mob seize Hôtel de Ville.—"Thanksgiving" in Paris.—Prices of Food.—Paris Rats.—Menagerie Meat.—Horse-meat.—Eatable only as Mince.—Government Interference.—Sorties.—Are Failures.—

Le Bourget taken by French.—Retaken by Prussians.—French Naval Officers.—Belleville National Guard.—Their Poetry.—Blundering.—Sheridan's Opinion of German Army .... Page 207

CHAPTER XVIII.

The National Guard.—Its Composition.—The American Ambulance.—Its Organization.—Its Success.—Dr. Swinburne, Chief Surgeon.—The Tent System.—Small Mortality.—Poor Germans in Paris.—Bombardment by Germans.—Wantonness of Artillery-men.—Bad News from the Loire.—"Le Plan Trochu."—St. Genevieve to appear.—Vinoy takes Command.—Paris surrenders.—Bourbaki defeated.—Attempts Suicide 221

CHAPTER XIX.

Election in France.—Terms of Peace.—Germans enter Paris.—Their Martial Appearance.—American Apartments occupied.—Washburne remonstrates.—Attitude of Parisians.—The Germans evacuate Paris.—Victualing the City.—Aid from England and the United States.—Its Distribution.—Sisters of Charity 234

CHAPTER XX.

The Commune.—Murder of French Generals.—The National Guard of Order.—It disbands.—The Reasons.—Flight of the Government to Versailles.—Thiers.—Attempts to reorganize National Guard.—An American arrested by Commune.—Legation intervenes.—His Discharge.—His Treatment.—Reign of King Mob.—"*Démonstrations Pacifiques.*"—Absurd Decrees of the Commune.—Destruction of the Vendôme Column 243

CHAPTER XXI.

Diplomatic Corps moves to Versailles.—Journey there and back.—Life at Versailles.—German Princes.—Battle at Clamart.—Unburied Insurgents.—Bitterness of Class Hatred.—Its Probable Causes.—United States Post-office at Versailles.—The Archbishop of Paris.—Attempts to save his Life.—Washburne's Kindness to him.—Blanqui.—Archbishop murdered.—Ultramontanism.—Bombardment by Government.—My Apartment struck.—Capricious Effects of Shells.—Injury to Arch of Triumph.—Bass-reliefs of Peace and War .... Page 256

CHAPTER XXII.

Reign of Terror.—Family Quarrels.—The Alsacians, etc., claim German Nationality.—They leave Paris on our Passes.—Prisoners of Commune.—Priests and Nuns.—Fragments of Shells.—"Articles de Paris."—Fearful Bombardment of "Point du Jour."—Arrest of Cluseret.—Commune Proclamations.—Capture of Paris.—Troops enter by Undefended Gate.—Their Slow Advance.—Fight at the Tuileries Gardens.—Communist Women.—Capture of Barricades.—Cruelties of the Troops.—"Pétroleuses."—Absurd Stories about them.—Public Buildings fired.—Destruction of Tuileries, etc., etc.—Narrow Escape of Louvre.—Treatment of Communist Prisoners.—Presents from Emperor of Germany..................... 271

CAMP, COURT, AND SIEGE.

CHAPTER I.

Hatteras.—"Black Drink."—Fortress Monroe.—General Butler.—Small-pox.—"L'Isle des Chats."—Lightning.—Farragut.—Troops land.—Surrender of Forts.

In February, 1862, the writer of the following pages, an officer on the staff of Brigadier-general Thomas Williams, was stationed at Hatteras. Of all forlorn stations to which the folly and wickedness of the Rebellion condemned our officers, Hatteras was the most forlorn. It blows a gale of wind half the time. The tide runs through the inlet at the rate of five miles an hour. It was impossible to unload the stores for Burnside's expedition during more than three days of the week. After an easterly blow—and there are enough of them—the waters are so piled up in the shallow sounds between Hatteras and the Main, that the tide ebbs without intermission for twenty-four hours.

The history of Hatteras is curious. There can be little doubt that English navigators penetrated into those waters long before the Pilgrims landed at Plymouth. But the colony was not a success. Of the colonists some returned to England; others died of want. The present inhabitants of the island are a sickly, puny race, the descendants of English convicts. When Great Britain broke up her penal settlement at the Bermudas, she transported the most hardened convicts to Van Diemens Land; those who had been convicted of minor offenses, she turned loose upon our coast. Here they intermarried; for the inhabitants of the Main look down upon them as an inferior race, and will have no social intercourse with them. The effect of these intermarriages is seen in the degeneracy of the race.

Until within a few years their principal occupation was wrecking. Hatteras lies on the direct route of vessels bound from the West Indies to Baltimore, Philadelphia, and New York. The plan adopted by these guileless natives to aid the storm in insuring a wreck was simple, but effective. There is a half-wild pony bred upon the island called "marsh pony." One of these animals was caught, a leg tied up Rarey fashion, a lantern slung to his neck, and the animal driven along the beach on a stormy night. The effect was that of a vessel riding at anchor. Other vessels approached, and were soon unpleasantly aware of the difference between a ship and a marsh pony.

The dwellings bear witness to the occupation of their owners. The fences are constructed of ships' knees and planks. In their parlors you may see on one side a rough board door, on the other an exquisitely finished rose-wood or mahogany cabin door, with silver or porcelain knobs. Contrast reigns everywhere.

But the place is not without its attractions to the botanist. A wild vine, of uncommon strength and toughness, grows abundantly, and is used in the place of rope. The iron-tree, hard enough to turn the edge of the axe, and heavy as the metal from which it takes its name, is found in abundance, and the tea-tree, from whose leaves the inhabitants draw their tea when the season has been a bad one for wrecks. This tea-tree furnishes the "black drink," which the Florida Indians drank to make themselves invulnerable. They drank it with due religious ceremonies till it nauseated them, when it was supposed to have produced the desired effect. What a pity that we can not associate some such charming superstition with the *maladie de mer!* It would so comfort us in our affliction!

But we were not to stay long on this enchanted isle. Butler had organized his expedition against New Orleans, and it was now ready to sail. He had applied for Thomas Williams, who had been strongly recommended to him by Weitzel, Kenzel, and other regular officers of his staff. Early in March we received orders to report to Butler at Fortress Monroe. We took one of those rolling tubs they call "propellers," which did the service between the fortress and Hatteras for the Quartermaster's Department; and, after nearly rolling over two or three times, we reached Old Point. Here we found the immense steamer the *Constitution,* loaded with three regiments, ready to sail. Williams had hoped to have two or three days to run North and see his wife and children, whom he had not seen for months. But with him considerations of duty were before all others. He thought that three regiments should be commanded by a brigadier, and he determined to sail at once. It was a disappointment to us all. To him the loss was irreparable. He never saw his family again.

It has always appeared to me that General Butler has not received the credit to which he is entitled for the capture of New Orleans. Without him New Orleans would not have been taken in 1862, and a blow inflicted upon the Confederacy, which the London *Times* characterized as the heaviest it had yet received — "almost decisive." The writer has no sympathy with General Butler's extreme views, and no admiration for his *protégés;* but he was cognizant of the New Orleans expedition from its inception, he accompanied it on the day it set sail, he landed with it in New Orleans, he remained in that city or its neighborhood during the whole of Butler's command; and a sense of justice compels him to say that Butler originated the expedition, that he carried it through, under great and unexpected difficulties, that he brought it to a successful termination, and that his government of the city at that time, and under the peculiar circumstances, was simply admirable.

It is not perhaps generally known that it was Butler who urged this enterprise upon the President. He was answered that no troops could be spared; M'Clellan wanted them all for his advance upon Richmond. Butler thereupon offered to raise the troops himself, provided the Government would give him three old regiments. The President consented. The troops were raised in New England,

and three old regiments—the Fourth Wisconsin, the Sixth Michigan, and the Twenty-first Indiana—designated to accompany them. At the last moment M'Clellan opposed the departure of the Western troops, and even applied for the "New England Division." It was with some difficulty that, appealing to the President, and reminding him of his promise, Butler was able to carry out the design for which the troops had been raised.

We sailed from Old Point on the 6th of March with the three regiments I have named. We numbered three thousand souls in all on board. If any thing were wanting at this day to prove the efficacy of vaccination, our experience on board that ship is sufficient. We took from the hospital a man who had been ill with the small-pox. He was supposed to be cured. Two days out, his disease broke out again. The men among whom he lay were packed as close as herring in a barrel, yet but one took the disease. They had all been vaccinated within sixty days. I commend this fact to the attention of those parish authorities in England who still obstinately refuse to enforce the Vaccination Act.

Five days brought us, in perfect health, to Ship Island. Here was another Hatteras, with a milder climate, and no "black drink;" a low, sandy island in the Gulf, off Mobile. This part of the Gulf of Mexico was discovered and settled by the French. They landed on Ship Island, and called it "L'Isle des Chats," from the large number of raccoons they found there. Not being personally acquainted with that typical American, they took him for a species of cat, and named the island accordingly. From Ship Island and the adjacent coast, which they settled, the French entered Lake Borgne and Lake Pontchartrain, and so up the Amite River in their boats. They dragged their boats across the short distance which separates the upper waters of the Amite from the Mississippi, embarked upon the "Father of Waters," and sailed down the stream. Here they played a trick upon John Bull; for, meeting an English fleet coming up, the first vessels that ever entered the mouths of the Mississippi, they boarded them, claimed to be prior discoverers, and averred that they had left their ships above. There existed in those days an understanding among maritime nations that one should not interfere with the prior discoveries of another. The English thereupon turned, and the spot, a short distance below New Orleans, is to this day called "English Turn."

We remained at the "Isle of Cats" about six weeks — the life monotonous enough. The beach offered a great variety of shell-fish, devil-fish, horse-shoes, and sea-horses. An odd thing was the abundance of fresh, pure water. Dig a hole two feet deep anywhere in the sand on that low island, rising scarcely five feet above the sea, and in two hours it was filled with fresh water. After using it a week, it became brackish; when all it was necessary to do was to dig another hole.

When on Ship Island, I witnessed a curious freak of lightning. One night we had a terrible thunderstorm, such as one sees only in those southern latitudes. In a large circular tent, used as a guard-tent, eight prisoners were lying asleep, side by side. The sentry stood leaning against the tent-pole, the butt of the musket on the ground, the bayonet against his shoulder. The lightning struck the tent-pole, leaped to the bayonet, followed down the barrel, tearing the stock to splinters, but only slightly stunning the sentry. Thence it passed along the ground, struck the first prisoner, killing him; passed through the six inside men without injury to them; and off by the eighth man, killing him.

Finally, the expedition was complete. Stores,

guns, horses, all had arrived. Butler became impatient for the action of the navy. He went to the South-west Pass, where Farragut's fleet was lying, and urged his advance. Farragut replied that he had no coal. Butler answered that he would give him what he wanted, and sent him fifteen hundred tons. He had had the foresight to ballast his sailing ships with coal, and so had an ample supply. A week passed, and still the ships did not ascend the river. Again Butler went to the Pass, and again Farragut said that he had not coal enough — that once past the forts, he might be detained on the river, and that it would be madness to make the attempt unless every ship were filled up with coal. Once again Butler came to his aid, and gave him three thousand tons. We were naturally surprised that so vital an expedition should be neglected by the Navy Department. The opinion was pretty general among us that the expedition was not a favorite with the Department, and that they did not anticipate any great success from it. They were quite as surprised as the rest of the world when Farragut accomplished his great feat.

At length all was ready. The troops were embarked, and lay off the mouth of the river, waiting for the action of the fleet. Farragut, after an idle bombardment of three days by the mortar-boats, which he told us he had no confidence in, but which he submitted to in deference to the opinions of the Department and of Porter (the firing ceased, by-the-way, when it had set fire to the wooden barracks in Fort Jackson, and might have done some good if continued), burst through the defenses, silenced the forts, and ascended the river. It is not my province to describe this remarkable exploit. Its effect was magical. An exaggerated idea prevailed at that time of the immense superiority of land batteries over ships. One gun on shore, it was said, was equal to a whole ship's battery. The very small results obtained by the united English and French fleets during the Crimean war were quoted in proof. Those magnificent squadrons effected scarcely any thing, for the capture of Bomarsund was child's play to them. The English naval officers, proud of their service and its glorious history, were delighted to find that, when daringly led, ships could still do something against land batteries, and all England rang with Farragut's exploit.

The part played by the army in this affair was minor, but still important. Our engineer officers, who had assisted in building forts St. Philip and Jackson, knew the ground well. Under their guidance we embarked, first in light-draught gun-boats, then in barges, and made our way through the shallow waters of the Gulf, and up the bayou, till we landed at Quarantine, between Fort St. Philip and the city, cutting off all communication between them. As, in the stillness of an April evening, we made our slow way up the bayou amidst a tropical vegetation, festoons of moss hanging from the trees and drooping into the water, with the chance of being fired on at any moment from the dark swamp on either side, the effect upon the imagination was striking, and the scene one not easily forgotten.

Farragut had passed up the river, but the forts still held out, and the great body of the troops was below them. When, however, they found themselves cut off from any chance of succor, the men in Fort St. Philip mutinied, tied their officers to the guns, and surrendered. Fort Jackson followed the example. No doubt our turning movement had hastened their surrender by some days. I once suggested to Butler that we had hastened it by a week. "A month, a month, sir," he replied.

It was here they told us that the United States

flag had been hauled down from the Mint by a mob headed by that scoundrel Mumford, and dragged through the mud. I heard Butler swear by all that was sacred, that if he caught Mumford, and did not hang him, might he be hanged himself. He caught him, and he kept his oath. There never was a wiser act. It quieted New Orleans like a charm. The mob, who had assembled at the gallows fully expecting to hear a pardon read at the last moment, and prepared to create a riot if he were pardoned, slunk home like whipped curs.

CHAPTER II.

New Orleans.—Custom-house.—Union Prisoners.—The Calaboose.—
"Them Lincolnites."—The St. Charles.—"Grape-vine Telegraph."
—New Orleans Shop-keepers.—Butler and Soulé.—The Fourth
Wisconsin.—A New Orleans Mob.—Yellow Fever.

ON the evening of the 1st of May, 1862, the leading transports anchored off the city. Butler sent for Williams, and ordered him to land at once. Williams, like the thorough soldier he was, proposed to wait till morning, when he would have daylight for the movement, and when the other transports, with our most reliable troops, would be up. "No, sir," said Butler, "this is the 1st of May, and on this day we must occupy New Orleans, and the first regiment to land must be a Massachusetts regiment." So the orders were issued, and in half an hour the Thirty-first Massachusetts Volunteers and the Sixth Massachusetts Battery set foot in New Orleans.

As we commenced our march, Williams saw the steamer *Diana* coming up with six companies of the Fourth Wisconsin. He ordered a halt, and sent me with instructions for them to land at once, and fall into the rear of the column. I passed through the mob without difficulty, gave the orders, and we resumed our march. The general had directed that our route should be along the levee, where our right was protected by the gun-boats. Presently we found that the head of the column was turning up Julia Street. Williams sent to know why the change had been made. The answer came back that Butler was there, and had given orders to pass in front of the St. Charles Hotel, while the band played "Yankee Doodle," and "Picayune Butler's come to Town," if they knew it. They did not know it, unfortunately, so we had one unbroken strain of the martial air of "Yankee Doodle" all the way.

Arrived at the Custom-house late in the evening, we found the doors closed and locked. Williams said to me, "What would you do?" "Break the doors open," I replied. The general, who could not easily get rid of his old, regular-army habits, ordered "Sappers and miners to the front." No doubt the sappers and miners thus invoked would have speedily appeared had we had any, but two volunteer regiments and a battery of light artillery were the extent of our force that night. I turned to the adjutant of the Fourth Wisconsin, and asked if he had any axes in his regiment. He at once ordered up two or three men. We found the weakest-looking door, and attacked it. As we were battering it in, the major of the Thirty-first came up, and took an axe from one of the men. Inserting the edge in the crack near the lock, he pried it gently, and the door flew open. I said, "Major, you seem to understand this sort of thing." He replied, "Oh! this isn't the first door I have broken open, by a long shot. I was once foreman of a fire-company in Buffalo."

We entered the building with great caution, for the report had been spread that it was mined. The men of the Fourth Wisconsin had candles in their knapsacks; they always had every thing, those fellows! We soon found the meter, turned the gas on, and then proceeded to make ourselves comfortable for the night. I established myself in the postmaster's private room — the Post-office was in the Custom-house—with his table for my bed, and a package of rebel documents for a pillow. I do not remember what my dreams were that night. We took the letters from the boxes to preserve them, and piled them in a corner of my room. They were all subsequently delivered to their respective addresses.

Pretty well tired out with the labor and excitement of the day, I was just making myself tolerably comfortable for the night, when the officer of the day reported that a woman urgently desired to see the general on a matter of life or death. She was admitted. She told us that her husband was a Union man, that he had been arrested that day and committed to the "Calaboose," and that his life was in danger. The general said to her, "My good woman, I will see to it in the morning." "Oh, sir," she replied, "in the morning he will be dead! They will poison him." We did not believe much in the poison story, but it was evident that she did. Williams turned to me, and said, "Captain, have you a mind to look into this?" Of course I was ready, and ordering out a company of the Fourth Wisconsin, and asking Major Boardman, a daring officer of that regiment, to accompany me, I started for the Calaboose, guided by the woman. The streets were utterly deserted. Nothing was heard but the measured tramp of the troops as we marched along. Arrived at the Calaboose, I ordered the man I was in search of to be brought out. I questioned him, questioned the clerk and the jailer, became satisfied that he was arrested for political reasons alone, ordered his release, and took him with me to the Custom-house, for he was afraid to return home. Being on the spot, it occurred to me that it would be as well to see if there were other political prisoners in the prison. I had the books brought, and examined the entries. At last I thought I had discovered another victim. The entry read, "Committed as a suspicious character, and for holding communication with Picayune Butler's troops." I ordered the man before me. The jailer took down a huge bunch of keys, and I heard door after door creaking on its hinges. At last the man was brought out. I think I never saw a more villainous countenance. I asked him what he was committed for? He evidently did not recognize the Federal uniform, but took me for a Confederate officer, and replied that he was arrested for talking to "them Lincolnites." I told the jailer that I did not want that man—that he might lock him up again.

Having commenced the search for political prisoners, I thought it well to make thorough work of it; so I inquired if there were other prisons in the city. There was one in the French quarter, nearly two miles off; so we pursued our weary and solitary tramp through the city. My men evidently did not relish it. The prison was quiet, locked up for the night. We hammered away at the door till we got the officers up; went in, examined the books, found no entries of commitments except for crime; put the officers on their written oaths that no one was confined there except for crime; and so returned to our Post-office beds.

The next day was a busy one. Early in the morning I went to the St. Charles Hotel to make arrangements for lodging the general and his staff. With some difficulty I got in. In the rotunda of that fine building sat about a dozen rebels, looking as black as a thunder-cloud. I inquired for the proprietor or clerk in charge, and a young man stepped forward: "Impossible to accommodate us; hotel closed; no servants in the house." I said, "At all events, I will see your rooms." Going into one of them, he closed the door and whispered, "It would be as much as my life is worth, sir, to offer to accommodate you here. I saw a man knifed on Canal Street yesterday for asking a naval officer the time of day. But if you choose to send troops and open the hotel by force, why, we will do our best to make you comfortable." Returning to the rotunda, I found Lieutenant Biddle, who had accompanied me

—one of the general's aids—engaged in a hot discussion with our rebel friends. I asked him "What use in discussing these matters?" and, turning to the rebs, with appropriate gesture said, "We've got you, and we mean to hold you." "That's the talk," they replied; "we understand *that*." They told us that the rebel army was in sight of Washington, and that John Magruder's guns commanded the Capitol. Why they picked out Magruder particularly, I can not say. This news had come by telegraph. We used to call the rebel telegraphic lines "the grapevine telegraph," for their telegrams were generally circulated with the bottle after dinner.

The shop-keepers in New Orleans, when we first landed there, were generally of the opinion of my friend the hotel-clerk. A naval officer came to us one morning at the Custom-house, and said that the commodore wanted a map of the river; that he had seen the very thing, but that the shop-keeper refused to sell it, intimating, however, that if he were compelled to sell it, why then, of course, he couldn't help himself. We ordered out a sergeant and ten men. The officer got his map, and paid for it.

But Butler was not the man to be thwarted in this way. Finding this *parti pris* on the part of the shop-keepers, he issued an order that all shops must be opened on a certain day, or that he should put soldiers in, and sell the goods for account "of whom it might concern." On the day appointed they were all opened. So, too, with the newspapers. They refused to print his proclamation. An order came to us to detail half a dozen printers, and send them under a staff officer to the office of the *True Delta*, and print the proclamation. We soon found the men. From a telegraph-operator to a printer, bakers, engine-drivers, carpenters, and coopers, we had representatives of all the trades. This was in the early days of the war. Afterward the men were of an inferior class. The proclamation was printed, and the men then amused themselves by getting out the paper. Next morning it appeared as usual; this was enough. The editor soon came to terms, and the other journals followed suit.

On the 2d of May Butler landed and took quarters at the St. Charles. There has been much idle gossip about attempts to assassinate him, and his fears of it. In regard to the latter, he landed in New Orleans, and drove a mile to his hotel, with one staff officer, and one armed orderly only on the box. When his wife arrived in the city, he rode with one orderly to the levee, and there, surrounded by the crowd, awaited her landing. As regards the former, we never heard of any well-authenticated attempt to assassinate him, and I doubt if any was ever made.

That afternoon Butler summoned the municipal authorities before him to treat of the formal surrender of the city. They came to the St. Charles, accompanied by Pierre Soulé as their counsel. A mob collected about the hotel, and became turbulent. Butler was unprotected, and sent to the Custom-house for a company of "Massachusetts" troops. The only Massachusetts troops there were the Thirty-first, a newly raised regiment. They afterward became excellent soldiers, but at that time they were very young and very green. It so happened, too, that the only company available was composed of the youngest men of the regiment. They were ordered out. The officer in charge did not know the way to the St. Charles. No guide was at hand, so I volunteered to accompany them. We drew the troops up on Common Street, and I entered the hotel to report them to Butler. I found him engaged in a most animated discussion with Soulé. Both were able and eloquent men, but

Butler undoubtedly got the better of the argument. Perhaps the fact that he had thirteen thousand bayonets to back his opinions gave point to his remarks. Interrupting his discourse for a moment only, he said, "Draw the men up round the hotel, sir; and if the mob make the slightest disturbance, fire on them on the spot," and went on with the discussion. Returning to the street, I found the mob apostrophizing my youthful soldiers with, "Does your mother know you're out?" and like popular wit. It struck me that the inquiry was well addressed. I felt disposed to ask the same question. I reported the matter to Williams, and he thought that it would be well to counteract the effect. That evening he sent the band of the Fourth Wisconsin to play in front of the St. Charles, with the whole regiment, tall, stalwart fellows, as an escort. In a few minutes the mob had slunk away. An officer heard one *gamin* say to another, "Those are Western men, and they say they *do* fight like h———." One of the officers told me that his men's fingers itched to fire.

I suppose that all mobs are alike, but certainly the New Orleans mob was as cowardly as it was brutal. When we first occupied the Custom-house, they collected about us, and annoyed our sentries seriously.

The orders were to take no notice of what was said, but to permit no overt act. I was sitting one day in my office, the general out, when Captain Bailey, the officer who distinguished himself so much afterward in building the Red River dam—and a gallant fellow he was—rushed in, and said, "Are we to stand this?" I said, "What's the matter, Bailey?" He replied that "One of those d—d scoundrels has taken his quid from his mouth, and thrown it into the sentry's face." I said, "No; I don't think that we are to stand that: that seems to me an 'overt act.' Arrest him." Bailey rushed out, called to the guard to follow him, and, jumping into the crowd, seized the fellow by the collar, and jerked him into the lines. The guard came up and secured him. The mob fell back and scattered, and never troubled us from that day. The fellow went literally down upon his knees, and begged to be let off. We kept him locked up that night, and the next day discharged him. He laid it all to bad whisky.

As the course of this narrative will soon carry the writer from New Orleans into the interior, he takes this opportunity to say that he has often been assured by the rebel inhabitants, men and women of position and character, that never had New Orleans been so well governed, so clean, so orderly, and so healthy, as it was under Butler. He soon got rid of the "Plug-uglies" and other ruffian bands: some he sent to Fort Jackson, and others into the Confederacy. There was no yellow fever in New Orleans while we held it, showing as plainly as possible that its prevalence or its absence is simply a question of quarantine. (Butler had sworn he would hang the health officer if the fever got up.) Before we arrived there, the "back door," as it was called—the lake entrance to the city—was always open, and for five hundred dollars any vessel could come up. In 1861, when our blockade commenced, and during the whole of our occupation, yellow fever was unknown. In 1866 we turned the city over to the civil authorities. That autumn there were a few straggling cases, and the following summer the fever was virulent.

CHAPTER III.

Vicksburg.—River on Fire.—Baton Rouge.—Start again for Vicksburg.—The *Hartford.*—The Canal.—Farragut.—Captain Craven.—The *Arkansas.*—Major Boardman.—The *Arkansas* runs the Gauntlet.—Malaria.

ADMIRAL FARRAGUT was anxious, after the capture of New Orleans, to proceed at once against Mobile. I heard him say that, in the panic excited by the capture of New Orleans, Mobile would fall an easy prey. The Government, however, for political as well as military reasons, was anxious to open the Mississippi. Farragut was ordered against Vicksburg, and Williams, with two regiments and a battery, was sent to accompany and support him. When one reflects upon the great strength of Vicksburg, and the immense resources it afterward took to capture it, it seems rather absurd to have sent us against it with two regiments and a battery. The excursion, however, if it is to be looked upon in this light, was delightful. We had two fine river boats. The plantations along the banks were in the highest state of cultivation; the young cane, a few inches above the ground, of the most lovely green. Indeed, I know no more beautiful green than that of the young sugar-cane. Our flag had not been seen in those parts for over a year, and the joy of the negroes when they had an opportunity to exhibit it without fear of their overseers was quite touching. The river was very high, and as we floated along we were far above the level of the plantations, and looked down upon the negroes at work, and into the open windows of the houses. The effect of this to one unused to it—the water above the land—was very striking. Natchez, a town beautifully situated on a high bluff, was gay with the inhabitants who had turned out to see us. The ladies, with their silk dresses and bright parasols, and the negro women, with their gaudy colors, orange especially, which they affect so much, and which, by-the-way, can be seen at a greater distance than any other color I know of.

One often hears of "setting a river on fire," metaphorically speaking: I have seen it done literally. The Confederate authorities had issued orders to burn the cotton along the banks to prevent its falling into our hands. But as the patriotism of the owners naturally enough needed stimulating, vigilance committees were organized, generally of those planters whose cotton was safe at a distance. These men preceded us as we ascended the river; and burned their neighbors' cotton with relentless patriotism. The burning material was thrown into the stream, and floated on the surface a long time before it was extinguished. At night it was a very beautiful sight to see the apparently flaming water. We had to exercise some care to steer clear of the burning masses.

Arrived opposite Vicksburg, we boarded the flag-ship to consult for combined operations. We found Farragut holding a council of his captains, considering the feasibility of passing the batteries of Vicksburg as he had passed the forts. We apologized for our intrusion, and were about to withdraw, when he begged us to stay, and, turning to Williams, he said, "General, my officers oppose my running by Vicksburg as impracticable. Only one supports me. So I must give it up for the present. In ten days they will all be of my opinion; and then the difficulties will be much greater than they are now." It turned out as he had said. In a few days they were nearly all of his opinion, and he did it.

But we found no dry place for the soles of our

feet. "The water was down," as the Scotchmen say (down from the hills), and the whole Louisiana side of the river was flooded. It would have been madness to land on the Vicksburg side with two regiments only. Nothing could be done, and we returned to Baton Rouge, where, finding a healthy and important position, a United States arsenal, and Union men who claimed our protection, Williams determined to remain and await orders.

Here cotton was offered us, delivered on the levee, at three cents a pound. It was selling at one dollar in New York. I spoke to Williams about it, and he said that there was no law against any officer speculating in cotton or other products of the country (one was subsequently passed), but that he would not have any thing to do with it; and advised me not to. I followed his advice and example. A subsequent post-commander did not. He made eighty thousand dollars out of cotton, and then went home and was made a brigadier-general; I never knew why.

But the Government was determined to open the river at all hazards. Farragut was re-enforced. Butler was ordered to send all the troops he could spare. Davis was ordered down with the Upper Mississippi fleet. Early in June we started again for Vicksburg, with six regiments and two batteries. It was a martial and beautiful sight to see the long line of gun-boats and transports following each other in Indian file at regular intervals. Navy and army boats combined, we numbered about twenty sail— if I may apply that word to steamers. On our way up, the flag-ship, the famous *Hartford*, was nearly lost. She grounded on a bank in the middle of the river, and with a falling stream. Of course there was the usual talk about a rebel pilot; but no vessel with the draught of the *Hartford*, a sloop-of-war, had ever before ventured to ascend above New Orleans. The navy worked hard all the afternoon to release her, but in vain. The hawsers parted like packthread. I was on board when a grizzled quartermaster, the very type of an old man-of-warsman, came up to the commodore on the quarter-deck, and, pulling his forelock, reported that there was a six-inch hawser in the hold. Farragut ordered it up at once. Two of our army transports, the most powerful, were lashed together, the hawser passed round them, and slackened. They then started with a jerk. The *Hartford* set her machinery in motion, the gunboat lashed along-side started hers, and the old ship came off, and was swept down with the current. It required some seamanship to disentangle all these vessels.

We found that the waters had subsided since our last visit to Vicksburg, and so landed at Young's Point, opposite the town. Some years previously there had been a dispute between the State authorities of Louisiana and of Mississippi, and the Legislature of the former had taken steps to turn the river, and cut off Vicksburg by digging a canal across the peninsula opposite. This we knew, and decided to renew the attempt. We soon found traces of the engineers' work. The trees were cut down in a straight line across the Point. Here we set to work. Troops were sent to the different plantations both up and down the river, and the negroes pressed into the service. It was curious to observe the difference of opinion among the old river captains as to the feasibility of our plan. Some were sure that the river would run through the cut; others swore that it would not, and could not be made to. The matter was soon settled by the river itself; for it suddenly rose one night, filled up our ditch, undermined the banks, and in a few hours destroyed our labor of days. A somewhat careful observation of the Mississippi since has satisfied me that if a canal be cut where the stream impinges upon the bank, it will take to it as naturally as a duck does to water. But when the current strikes the opposite bank, as it does at Young's Point, you can not force it from its course. Had we attempted our canal some miles farther up, where the current strikes the right bank, we should have succeeded. Grant, the next year, renewed our ditch-digging experiment in the same place, and with infinitely greater resources, but with no better success.

Farragut had now made his preparations to run by the batteries. He divided his squadron into three divisions, accompanying the second division himself. The third was under command of Captain Craven, of the *Brooklyn*. We stationed Nim's light battery—and a good battery it was—on the point directly opposite Vicksburg, to assist in silencing the fire of one of the most powerful of the shore batteries. Very early in the morning Farragut got under way; two of his divisions passed, completely silencing the rebel batteries. The third division did not attempt the passage. This led to an angry correspondence between the commodore and Craven, and resulted in Craven's being relieved, and ordered to report to Washington. There was a great difference of opinion among naval officers as to Craven's conduct. He was as brave an officer as lived. He contended that it was then broad daylight, that the gunners on shore had returned to their guns, and that his feeble squadron would have been exposed to the whole fire of the enemy, without any adequate object to be gained in return. Farragut replied that his orders were to pass, and that he should have done it at all hazards.

And now an incident occurred which mortified the commodore deeply. His powerful fleet, re-enforced by Davis, lay above Vicksburg. The weather was intensely hot, and the commodore, contrary to his own judgment, as he told Williams, but on the urgent request of his officers, had permitted the fires to be extinguished. Early one morning we had sent a steamboat with a party up the river to press negroes into our canal work. Suddenly a powerful iron-clad, flying the Confederate colors, appeared coming out of the Yazoo River. There was nothing for our unarmed little boat to do but to run for it. The *Arkansas* opened from her bow-guns, and the first shell, falling among the men drawn up on deck, killed the captain of the company, and killed or wounded ten men. It is so rarely that a shell commits such havoc, that I mention it as an uncommon occurrence.

The firing attracted the attention of the fleet, and they beat to quarters. But there was no time to get up steam. The *Arkansas* passed through them all almost unscathed, receiving and returning their fire. The shells broke against her iron sides without inflicting injury. The only hurt she received was from the *Richmond*. Alden kept his guns loaded with powder only, prepared to use shell or shot as circumstances might require. He loaded with solid shot, and gave her a broadside as she passed. This did her some damage, but nothing serious.

In the mean time the alarm was given to the transports. Farragut had sent us an officer to say that the *Arkansas* was coming, that he should stop her if he could, but that he feared that he could not. The troops were got under arms, and our two batteries ordered to the levee. A staff officer said to General Williams, "General, don't let us be caught here like rats in a trap; let us attempt something, even if we fail." "What would you do?" said the general. "Take the *Laurel Hill*, put some picked men on board of her, and let us ram the rebel. We may not sink her, but we may disable or delay her, and help the gun-boats to capture her." "A good idea," said the general; "send for Major Boardman." Boardman, the daring officer to whom I have before referred, had been brought up as a midshipman. He was known in China as the "American devil," from a wild exploit there in scaling the walls of Canton one dark night when the gates were closed; climbing them with the help of his dagger only, making holes in the masonry for his hands and feet. He was afterward killed by guerrillas, having become colonel of his regiment. Boardman came; the *Laurel Hill* was cleared; twenty volunteers from the Fourth Wisconsin were put on board, and steam got up. The captain refused to go, and another transport captain was put in command. We should have attempted something, perhaps failed; but I think one or other of us would have been sunk. But our preparations were all in vain. The *Arkansas* had had enough of it for that day. She rounded to, and took refuge under the guns of Vicksburg.

Reporting this incident to Butler subsequently, he said, "You would have sunk her, sir; you would have sunk her."

Farragut, as I have said, was deeply mortified. He gave orders at once to get up steam, and prepared to run the batteries again, determined to destroy the rebel ram at all hazards. He had resolved to ram her with the *Hartford* as she lay under the guns of Vicksburg. It was with great difficulty he was dissuaded from doing so, and only upon the promise of Alden that he would do it for him in the *Richmond*. Farragut, in his impulsive way, seized Alden's hand, "Will you do this for me, Alden? will you do it?" The rapidity of the current, the unusual darkness of the night, and the absence of lights on the *Arkansas* and on shore, prevented the execution of the plan. To finish with the *Arkansas*, she afterward came down the river to assist in the attack on Baton Rouge. Part of her machinery gave out; she turned and attempted to return to Vicksburg, was pursued by our gun-boats, run ashore, abandoned, and burned.

The rebels never had any luck with their gun-boats. They always came to grief. They were badly built, badly manned, or badly commanded. The *Louisiana*, the *Arkansas*, the *Manassas*, the *Tennessee*, the *Albemarle* — great things were expected of them all, and they did nothing.

But we were as far from the capture of Vicksburg as ever. Fever attacked our men in those fatal swamps, and they became thoroughly discouraged. The sick-list was fearful. Of a battery of eighty men, twenty only were fit for duty. The Western troops, and they were our best, were homesick. Lying upon the banks of the Mississippi, with transports above Vicksburg convenient for embarkation, they longed for home. The colonels came to Williams, and suggested a retreat *up* the river, to join Halleck's command. Williams held a council of war. He asked me to attend it. The colonels gave their opinions, some in favor of, and others against, the proposed retreat. When it came to my turn, I spoke strongly against it. I urged that we had no *right* to abandon our comrades at New Orleans; that it might lead to the recapture of that city; that if our transports were destroyed, we should at least attempt to get back by land. I do not suppose that Williams ever entertained the least idea of retreating up the river, but thought it due to his officers to hear what they had to say in favor of it. The plan was abandoned.

CHAPTER IV.

Sickness.—Battle of Baton Rouge.—Death of Williams.—"Fix Bayonets!"—Thomas Williams.—His Body.—General T. W. Sherman.—Butler relieved.—General Orders, No. 10.—Mr. Adams and Lord Palmerston.—Butler's Style.

Of the events which immediately followed the council of war referred to in the last chapter, the writer knows only by report. He was prostrated with fever, taken to a house on shore, moved back to head-quarters boat, put on board a gun-boat, and sent to New Orleans. Farragut, with his usual kindness, offered to take him on board the *Hartford*, give him the fleet-captain's cabin, and have the fleet-surgeon attend him. But Williams declined the offer. Farragut then offered to send him to New Orleans in a gun-boat. This Williams accepted. The writer was taken to New Orleans, sent to military hospital, an assistant-surgeon's room given up to him, and every care lavished upon him; for one of Williams's staff—poor De Kay—wounded in a skirmish, had died in hospital. Butler had conceived the idea—erroneous, I am sure—that he had been neglected by the surgeons. When I was brought down he sent them word that if another of Williams's staff died there, they would hear from him. I did not die.

Meantime, unable to effect any thing against Vicksburg, with more than half his men on the sick-list, Williams returned to Baton Rouge. The rebel authorities, with spies everywhere, heard of the condition of our forces, and determined to attack them. Early one foggy morning twelve thousand men, under Breckenridge, attacked our three or four thousand men fit for duty. But they did not catch Williams napping. He had heard of the intended movement, and was prepared to meet it. Our forces increased, too, like magic. Sick men in hospital, who thought that they could not stir hand or foot, found themselves wonderfully better the moment there was a prospect of a fight. Happily a thick mist prevailed. Happily, too, they first attacked the Twenty-first Indiana, one of our stanchest regiments, holding the centre of the position. This fine regiment was armed with breech-loaders, the only ones in the Gulf. Lying on the ground, they could see the legs of the rebels below the mist, and fire with a steady aim upon them, themselves unseen. On the right the Thirtieth Massachusetts was engaged, but not hotly. The left was but slightly pressed. Williams had carefully reconnoitred the ground the afternoon before, and marked out his different positions. As the battle progressed, he fell back upon his second position, contracting his lines. As it grew hotter, he issued orders to fall back upon the third position. As he gave the order, the lieutenant-colonel of the Twenty-first, Colonel Keith, as plucky a little fellow as lived, came to him and said, "For God's sake, general, don't order us to fall back! We'll hold this position against the whole d—d rebel army." "Do your men feel that way, colonel?" replied Williams; and turning to the regiment, he said, "Fix bayonets!" As he uttered these words, he was shot through the heart. The men fixed bayonets, charged, and the rebels gave way. But there was no one competent to take command. The Fourth Wisconsin, on our left, waited in vain for the orders Williams had promised them, eager to advance, for he had meant that this regiment should take the rebels in flank. The victory was won, but its fruits were not gathered.

I think that grander words were never uttered by

a commander on the field of battle as he received his death-wound than these words of Williams's. "Fix bayonets!" means business, and in this instance they meant victory.

Thomas Williams was a noble fellow. Had he lived, he would have been one of the great generals of our war. Butler told the writer that, had Williams survived Baton Rouge, it was his intention to have turned over the whole military command to him, and confined himself to civil matters. The "General Order" he issued on Williams's death is a model of classic and pathetic English. It is quoted as such by Richard Grant White in his "Miscellany." I give it entire, for it can not be too widely circulated, both on account of its style and its subject.

"Head-quarters, Department of the Gulf,
"New Orleans, August 7th, 1862.

"GENERAL ORDERS, No. 56:

"The commanding general announces to the Army of the Gulf the sad event of the death of Brigadier-general Thomas Williams, commanding Second Brigade, in camp at Baton Rouge.

"The victorious achievement, the repulse of the division of Major-general Breckenridge by the troops led on by General Williams, and the destruction of the mail-clad *Arkansas* by Captain Porter, of the navy, is made sorrowful by the fall of our brave, gallant, and successful fellow-soldier.

"General Williams graduated at West Point in 1837; at once joined the Fourth Artillery in Florida, where he served with distinction; was thrice breveted for gallant and meritorious services in Mexico as a member of General Scott's staff. His life was that of a soldier devoted to his country's service. His country mourns in sympathy with his wife and children, now that country's care and precious charge.

"We, his companions in arms, who had learned to love him, weep the true friend, the gallant gentleman, the brave soldier, the accomplished officer, the pure patriot and victorious hero, and the devoted Christian. All, and more, went out when Williams died. By a singular felicity, the manner of his death illustrated each of these generous qualities.

"The chivalric American gentleman, he gave up the vantage of the cover of the houses of the city, forming his lines in the open field, lest the women and children of his enemies should be hurt in the fight.

"A good general, he made his dispositions and prepared for battle at the break of day, when he met his foe!

"A brave soldier, he received the death-shot leading his men!

"A patriot hero, he was fighting the battle of

his country, and died as went up the cheer of victory!

"A Christian, he sleeps in the hope of a blessed Redeemer!

"His virtues we can not exceed; his example we may emulate, and, mourning his death, we pray, 'May our last end be like his.'

"The customary tribute of mourning will be worn by the officers in the department.

"By command of Major-general BUTLER.

"R. T. DAVIS, Captain and A. A. A. G."

Williams was an original thinker. He had some rather striking ideas about the male portion of the human race. He held that all men were by nature cruel, barbarous, and coarse, and were only kept in order by the influence of women—their wives, mothers, and sisters. "Look at those men," he would say. "At home they are respectable, law-abiding citizens. It's the women who make them so. Here they rob hen-roosts, and do things they would be ashamed to do at home. There is but one thing will take the place of their women's influence, and that is discipline; and I'll give them enough of it." I used to think his views greatly exaggerated, but I came to be very much of his opinion before the war was over.

A curious thing happened to his body. It was sent down in a transport with wounded soldiers. She came in collision with the gunboat *Oneida* coming up, and was sunk. Various accounts were given of the collision. It was of course reported that the rebel pilot of the transport had intentionally run into the gun-boat. I think this improbable, for I have observed that rebel pilots value their lives as much as other people. Captain (afterward Admiral) Lee lay by the wreck, and picked up the wounded: none were lost. Shortly afterward Gun-boat No. 1, commanded by Crosby, a great friend of Williams, came up. Lee transferred the men to her, ordered her to New Orleans, and himself proceeded to Baton Rouge. Crosby heard that Williams's body was on board. He spent several hours in searching for it, but without success. He reluctantly concluded to abandon the search. Some hours later in the day, and several miles from the scene of the disaster, a piece of the wreck was seen floating down the current, with a box upon it. A boat was lowered, and the box was picked up. It turned out to be the coffin containing the body. His portmanteau too floated ashore, fell into honest hands, and was returned to me by a gentleman of the coast.

It had been General Butler's intention, on my recovery, to give me command of the Second Louisiana, a regiment he was raising in New Orleans, mostly from disbanded and rebel soldiers. My recovery was so long delayed, however, that he was compelled to fill the vacancy otherwise. Shortly afterward General T. W. Sherman was ordered to New Orleans, and I was assigned to duty on his staff. He was sent to Carondelet to take charge of the post at the Parapet, and of all the northern approaches to New Orleans. This was done under orders from Washington; but of this Sherman was not aware, for no copy of the orders had been sent him. He never knew to what an important command it was the intention of the Government to assign him till some years later, when the writer, having become Adjutant-general of the Department of the Gulf, found the orders in the archives of the Department.

But the days of Butler's command were brought to a close. Banks arrived with re-enforcements, and exhibited his orders to take command of the Department. No one was more surprised than Butler. He had supposed that Banks's expedition was directed against Texas. His recall seemed ungrateful on the part of the Government, for it was to him that the capture of New Orleans at that early date was principally due. It is probable that the consuls in that city had complained of him, and our Government, thinking it all-important to give no cause of complaint to foreign governments, Great Britain and France especially, recalled him.

As General Butler will not again appear in these pages, I can not close this part of my narrative without endeavoring to do him justice in regard to one or two points on which he has been attacked. The silver-spoon story is simply absurd. Butler confiscated and used certain table-silver. When Banks relieved him, he turned it over to him. When a howl was made about it toward the close of the war, and the Government referred the papers to Butler, for a report, he simply forwarded a copy of Banks's quarter-master's receipt. I was amused once at hearing that inimitable lecturer, Artemus Ward, get off a joke upon this subject in New Orleans. He was describing the Mormons, and a tea-party at Brigham Young's, and said that Brigham Young probably had a larger tea-service than any one in the world, "except," said he, and then paused as if to reflect—"except, perhaps, General Butler." Imagine the effect upon a New Orleans audience. It is perhaps needless to observe that Butler was not at that time in command.

The only charge against Butler which was never thoroughly disproved was that he permitted those about him to speculate, to the neglect of their duties and to the injury of our cause and good name. He must have been aware of these speculations, and have shut his eyes to them. But that he himself profited pecuniarily by them, I do not believe.

The famous General Orders, No. 10, "The Woman's Order," was issued while I was in New Orleans, and excited much and unfavorable comment. Butler ordered that ladies insulting United States officers should be treated "as women of the town plying their trade." Strong, his adjutant-general, remonstrated, and begged him to alter it. He said that he meant simply that they should be arrested and punished according to the municipal law of the city, *i. e.*, confined for one night and fined five dollars. Strong replied, "Why not say so, then?" But Butler has much of the vanity of authorship. He was pleased with the turn of the phrase, thought it happy, and refused to surrender it.

In this connection, when in London, I heard an anecdote of Mr. Adams and Lord Palmerston which is not generally known. It was not often that any one got the better of old "Pam," but Mr. Adams did. When Butler's order reached England, Lord Palmerston was the head of the Government; Lord John Russell was Secretary of State for Foreign Affairs. Lord Palmerston wrote to Mr. Adams to know if the order as printed in the London papers was authentic. Mr. Adams asked if he inquired officially or privately. Lord Palmerston replied rather evasively. Mr. Adams insisted. Lord Palmerston answered that if Mr. Adams must know, he begged him to understand that he inquired officially. Mr. Adams had the correspondence carefully copied in Moran's best handwriting, and inclosed it to Lord John with a note inquiring, who was Her Majesty's Secretary of State for Foreign Affairs; was it Lord Palmerston, or was it Lord John? A quick reply came from Lord John, asking him to do nothing further in the matter till he heard from him again. The next day a note was received from Lord Palmerston withdrawing the correspondence.

I have given two specimens of Butler's style. Here is another, and of a different character. At the request of a naval officer in high command, Farragut applied to Butler for steamboats to tow the mortar vessels to Vicksburg. Butler replied that he regretted that he had none to spare. The officer answered that if Butler would prevent his brother from sending quinine and other contraband stores into the Confederacy, there would be boats enough. This came to Butler's ears. He answered. After giving a list of his boats, and stating their different employments, he proceeded substantially as follows. I quote from memory. "Now, there are two kinds of lying. The first is when a man deliberately states what he knows to be false. The second is when he states what is really false, but what at the time he believes to be true. For instance, when Captain —— reports that the ram *Louisiana* came down upon his gun-boats, and a desperate fight ensued, he stated what is in point of fact false; for the *Louisiana* was blown up and abandoned, and was drifting with the current, as is proved by the report of the rebel commander, Duncan: but Captain —— believed it to be true, and acted accordingly; for he retreated to the mouth of the river, leaving the transports to their fate."

CHAPTER V.

T. W. Sherman. — Contrabands. — Defenses of New Orleans. — Exchange of Prisoners. — Amenities in War. — Port Hudson. — Reconnoissance in Force. — The Fleet. — Our Left. — Assault of May 27th. — Sherman wounded. — Port Hudson surrenders.

THE autumn of 1862 passed without any special incident. Sherman rebuilt the levees near Carrollton, repaired and shortened the Parapet, pushed his forces to the north, and occupied and fortified Manchac Pass. All these works were constructed by Captain Bailey, to whom I have already alluded, and of whom I shall have much to say hereafter; for he played a most important and conspicuous part in the Louisiana campaigns. At Manchac he constructed a *bijou* of a work built of mud and clamshells. He had the most remarkable faculty of making the negroes work. I have seen the old inhabitants of the coast (French *côte*, bank of the river) stopping to gaze with surprise at the "niggers" trundling their wheelbarrows filled with earth on the double-quick. Such a sight was never before seen in Louisiana, and probably never will be again. Sherman was the first officer, too, to enroll the blacks, set them to work, and pay them wages. He was no *professed* friend of the negro, but he did more practically for their welfare to make them useful, and save them from vagabondage, than Phelps or any other violent abolitionist, who said that the slaves had done enough work in their day, and so left them in idleness, and fed them at their own tables. Every negro who came within our lines— and there were hundreds of them—was enrolled on the quartermaster's books, clothed, fed, and paid wages, the price of his clothing being deducted. The men worked well. They were proud of being paid like white men.

Later in the season, Sherman sent out successful expeditions into the enemy's territory. One to Ponchitoula destroyed a quantity of rebel government stores; another, across Lake Pontchartrain, captured a valuable steamer. Sherman employed an admirable spy, the best in the Department. As a rule, both Butler's and Banks's spies were a poor lot, constantly getting up cock-and-bull stories to magnify their own importance, and thus misled their employers. Sherman's spy was a woman. Her information always turned out to be reliable, and, what is perhaps a little remarkable, was never exaggerated.

Butler had now left the Department, and Banks was in command. About this time Holly Springs was occupied by Van Dorn, and our dépôts burned, Grant falling back. The attack upon Vicksburg, too, from the Yazoo River had failed. Banks's spies exaggerated these checks greatly, and reported that the enemy was in full march upon New Orleans. There was something of a stampede among us. A new command was created, called the "Defenses of New Orleans," and given to Sherman. In a fortnight the face of these defenses was vastly changed. When he took command, the city was undefended to the east and south. In a few days the rebel works were rebuilt, guns mounted, light batteries stationed near the works, each supported by a regiment of infantry. New Orleans, with our gun-boats holding the river and lake, was impregnable.

No commanding officer in our army was more thorough in his work than Sherman. I remember an instance of this in an exchange of prisoners which took place under his orders. The arrangements were admirable. We were notified that a schooner with United States soldiers on board lay at Lakeport, on Lake Pontchartrain. Within an hour of receiving the report I was on my way to effect the exchange. I was accompanied by our quartermaster, to insure prompt transportation to New Orleans; by our commissary, to see that the men were fed, for our prisoners were always brought in with very insufficient supplies, the rebel officers assuring us that they had not food to give them; and by our surgeon, to give immediate medical assistance to those requiring it. Sherman told me to give the rebel officers in charge a breakfast or dinner, and offered to pay his share. We reached Lakeport about sunset. I went on board at once, and made arrangements for the exchange at six o'clock in the morning. I inquired of the men if they had had any thing to eat. "Nothing since morning." The officer in charge explained that they had been delayed by head-winds; but they were always delayed by head-winds. We sent food on board that night. At six in the morning the schooner was warped along-side of the pier. A train was run down, a line of sentries posted across the pier, and no stranger permitted to approach. The roll was called, and as each man answered to his name, he stepped ashore and entered the train. Meantime I had ordered down a breakfast from the famous French restaurant at Lakeport; and while the necessary arrangements were being completed by the quartermaster, we gave the Confederate officers a breakfast. It was easy to see, from the manner in which they attacked it, that they did not fare so sumptuously every day. Colonel Szymanski, who commanded, an intelligent and gentlemanly officer, asked permission to buy the remnants from the restaurant for lunch and dinner on the return voyage. The train was now ready, the schooner set sail, and we started for New Orleans. On our arrival, we bought out a baker's shop and one or two orange-women. It was a long time since the prisoners had tasted white bread. They formed, and marched to the barracks. Before noon that day they were in comfortable quarters, and seated at a bountiful dinner, prepared in advance for them. This was Sherman's organization. I had an opportunity to contrast it, not long after, with an exchange effected under direct orders from head-quarters. The contrast was not in Banks's favor.

On this occasion I had gone down as a spectator, and to see if I could be of use. I was going on board the cartel, when I was stopped by a lady who asked me to take a young girl on board to see her brother. Of course I was compelled to refuse. She then asked if I would not tell her brother that she was on the end of the pier, that they might at least see each other. This I promised to do. On board I found a number of sailors, part of the crew of the *Mississippi*, which had been recently lost at Port Hudson. As usual, they had had nothing to eat since the previous evening.

Before leaving the vessel, I inquired for Lieutenant Adams. They told me that he was in "that boat," pointing to one, having pulled ashore, hoping to see his sister. As I approached the shore I met his boat returning; I stopped it, and asked him if he had seen his sister. He had not. I told him to get in with me, and I would take him to her. He did so, and I pulled to within a few yards of the spot where she was standing. Scarcely a word passed between them, for both were sobbing. We remained there about three minutes, and then pulled back. We were all touched, officers and men, by this little display of the home affections in the midst of war. I think it did us all good.

General Banks was not pleased when he heard of this incident. Perhaps it was reported to him incorrectly. But Sherman thought that I had done right. I always found that our regular officers were more anxious to soften the rigors of war, and to avoid all unnecessary severity, than our volunteers. On our march through Louisiana under Franklin, a strong provost guard preceded the column, whose duty it was to protect persons and property from stragglers till the army had passed. If planters in the neighborhood applied for a guard, it was always furnished. On one occasion such a guard was captured by guerrillas. General Franklin wrote at once to General Taylor, protesting against the capture of these men as contrary to all the laws of civilized warfare. Taylor promptly released them, and sent them back to our lines. General Lee did the same in Virginia.

And so the winter wore through, and the spring came. Banks made a successful expedition to Alexandria, winning the battle of Irish Bend. I am the more particular to record this, as his reputation as a commander rests rather upon his success in retreat than in advance. And the month of May found us before Port Hudson.

Vicksburg is situated eight hundred miles above New Orleans. In all this distance there are but five commanding positions, and all these on the left or east bank of the river. It was very important to the rebels to fortify a point below the mouth of the Red River, in order that their boats might bring forward the immense supplies furnished by Louisiana, Texas, and Arkansas. They selected Port Hudson, a miserable little village not far below the Red River, and fortified it strongly. Sherman had seen the importance of attacking this place when the works were commenced, but Butler told him, very truly, that he had not troops enough in the Department to justify the attempt.

I think that it was the 24th of May when we closed in upon Port Hudson. Sherman's command held the left. He had a front of three miles, entirely too much for one division. The country was a *terra incognita* to us, and we had to feel our way. Of course there was much reconnoitring to be done — exciting and interesting work — but not particularly safe or comfortable. Sherman did much of this himself. He had a pleasant way of riding up in full sight of the enemy's batteries, accompanied by his staff. Here he held us while he criticised the manner in which the enemy got his guns ready to open on us. Presently a shell would whiz over our heads, followed by another somewhat nearer. Sherman would then quietly remark, "They are getting the range now: you had better scatter." As a rule we did not wait for a second order.

I remember his sending out a party one day to reconnoitre to our extreme left, and connect with the fleet, which lay below Port Hudson. We knew it was somewhere there; but how far off it lay, or what was the character of the country between us, we did not know. A company of cavalry reconnoitring in the morning had been driven in. Sherman determined to make a reconnoissance in force. He sent out the cavalry again, and supported it with a regiment of infantry. I asked permission to accompany them. He gave it, and added, "By-the-way, captain, when you are over there, just ride up and draw their fire, and see where their guns are. They won't hit you." I rode up and drew their fire, and they did not hit me; but I don't recommend the experiment to any of my friends.

This reconnoissance was successful. We passed through a thickly wooded country, intersected by small streams, for about two miles, when we emerged upon the open in full view of the works of Port Hudson. This we had to cross, exposed to their fire. We thus gained the road, running along the top of the bluff; and, following this, we came in view of the fleet. Our arrival produced a sensation. They had been looking out for us for two or three days. The men swarmed up the rigging and on to the yards. Fifty telescopes were leveled at us; and as we galloped down the bluff and along the levee to the ships, cheer after cheer went up from the fleet. We went on board the nearest gun-boat, and got some bread-and-cheese and Bass—which tasted remarkably good, by-the-way. I staid but a little while, for I was anxious about my men. On our homeward march the enemy opened on us, and we lost two or three men. I felt saddened at the loss of any men while in some measure under my command, and reported this loss first to the general. I was much comforted when he replied, "Lose men! of course you lost men. Reconnoissances in force always lose men!"

A few weeks previous to my visit to the fleet, Farragut had attempted to run by Port Hudson, with a view to communicate with Porter at Vicksburg, but more especially to blockade the mouth of the Red River. This, though the least known of his great exploits, was probably the most perilous and the least successful. But two vessels passed the batteries — his own, the old *Hartford*, as a matter of course, and the gun-boat that was lashed to her. Several were driven back disabled, and that fine ship, the *Mississippi*, got aground and was lost. The *Hartford* and her consort, however, did good service, preventing all rebel vessels from showing themselves upon the river between Port Hudson and Vicksburg.

While on board the gun-boat, I remarked to her captain that I was surprised that General Banks did not make his assault upon our left, where we could have the aid of the fleet, instead of on the right, as he evidently proposed to do. The remark was repeated to Farragut, who mentioned it to Banks. A day or two after the failure of our assault of the 27th of May, I was surprised by a summons to head-quarters, and still more surprised when I was asked what was my plan for taking Port Hudson. My plan was simply to utilize our powerful fleet instead of ignoring it. Sherman, who, after his recovery from his wound received a few days later, visited the place after its fall, and carefully examined the ground, told me that the assault should undoubtedly have been made on our left, not only on account of the fleet, but on account of the character of the ground.

We afterward erected batteries here within a very short distance of the enemy's, and commanding them; and we dug up to their very citadel. Had another assault been ordered, as it seemed at one time probable, it would have been made here, and would probably have been a repetition, on a small scale, of the affair of the Malakoff. There was another advantage on this flank. Had we effected a lodgment even with a small force, we could have maintained our position in the angle between the parapet and the river until re-enforcements reached us. At the points selected for the assault of the 27th of May—had we succeeded in getting in—we should have found ourselves exposed to attacks in front and on both flanks, and should probably have been driven out again.

The siege of Port Hudson was tedious and bloody. Banks ordered an assault. It was made, and resulted in a miserable repulse. He was asked why assault when the place must inevitably be starved out in a few weeks. He replied, "The people of the North demand blood, sir." Sherman led the assault in person, at the head of the Sixth Michigan regiment; Bailey headed the negroes, with plank and other materials to fill up the fosse. I had heard before of negroes turning white from fright, and did not believe it; but it is literally true. The men advanced within a few yards of the works, but could effect no lodgment. There never was a more useless waste of life. Sherman lost his leg, and his horse was killed under him; one staff officer and his horse were killed; an orderly was killed; another staff officer was wounded, and his horse killed; and another orderly had his horse killed. This is a pretty bloody ten minutes' work for a general and his staff.

The staff officer who was wounded was Badeau, our consul-general at London, and author of that model military history, the first volume of the "Life of Grant."

Fortunately, probably, for me, I had been sent with orders to Sherman's other brigade, to support the attack by an assault on the left. It was hot enough where I was. The shells shrieked over my head, and a round shot rolled playfully between my horse's legs. But it was nothing like the "hell of fire" to which Sherman was exposed.

Sherman having been sent to New Orleans, to hospital, General William Dwight took command of the division. After a while another assault was made: it was as fruitless as the first. But the enemy was now getting short of provisions. They lived mostly on Indian corn. Many deserters came to us, mostly Louisianians, for the "Wrackensackers" (Arkansas men) and the Texans rarely deserted. These made up the garrison. They reported great want in the place; and, what was far better proof — for it will not do to trust implicitly to deserters' stories—their gums showed the want of proper food. The end was approaching. On the 4th of July Vicksburg surrendered. Our outposts communicated this intelligence to the rebel outposts, and chaffed them about it. The news was reported to Gardiner. He sent a flag to Banks to inquire if it were true. Banks replied that it was, and Port Hudson surrendered.

It was curious to observe the sort of *entente cordiale* which the soldiers on both sides established during the siege. When they were tired of trying to pick each other off through the loop-holes, one of them would tie a white handkerchief to his bayonet, and wave it above the parapet. Pretty soon a handkerchief, or its equivalent—for the rebs did not indulge in useless luxuries—would be seen waving on the other side. This meant truce. In a moment the men would swarm out on both sides, sitting with their legs dangling over the parapet, chaffing each other, and sometimes with pretty rough wit. They were as safe as if a regular flag were out. No man dared to violate this tacit truce. If he had done so, his own comrades would have dealt roughly with him. After a while, on one side or the other, some one would cry out, "Get under cover now, Johnnie," or "Look out now, Yank; we are going to fire," and the fire would recommence.

Active military operations were now suspended, and I obtained leave of absence. But it was revoked; for General William B. Franklin had arrived in the Department, and I was assigned to his staff. I naturally felt disappointed at losing my leave, but I was subsequently glad that it had so happened; for it led to my promotion, and to the establishment of friendly and pleasant relations which have survived the war.

CHAPTER VI.

Major-general Franklin.—Sabine Pass.—Collision at Sea.—March through Louisiana.—Rebel Correspondence.—"The Gypsy's Wassail."—Rebel Women.—Rebel Poetry.—A Skirmish.—Salt Island.—Winter Climate.—Banks's Capua.—Major Joseph Bailey.

EARLY in the fall of 1863, Major-general Franklin was put in command of the military part of an expedition which had been planned against Sabine Pass, on the coast of Texas. The arrangement was for the navy to enter the port at night, get in the rear of the work, and capture it; whereupon the troops were to land, garrison the place, and hold it as a base for future operations in Texas. The plan failed. The expected signals were not displayed. The gunboats made the attempt in broad daylight, got aground in the shallow and winding channel, and were captured. Many of the sailors jumped overboard, swam ashore, ran down through the marsh, and were picked up by our boats. The plan had failed, and there was nothing for the troops to do but to return.

That night we had a collision between one of our large sea-going steamers and our light river boat used for head-quarters. Our side was apparently smashed in. A panic seized the crew; captain, pilot, engineer, hands, all rushed for the steamer. Most of our head-quarters company and officers followed the example. I was reading in the cabin when the collision occurred. The crash and the cries attracted my attention. I went upon deck, and tried for a moment to restore order, but in vain. The soldiers on the steamer shouted, "Come on board! come on board! You're sinking! there's a great hole in your side!" The waves dashed our little boat against the sides of the steamer, and the light plank of the wheel-house was grinding and crashing. I can easily understand how contagious is a panic. It was with a great effort I could restrain myself from following the example set me. I knew, however, that my place was with the general, and I went in search of him. I found him on the hurricane-deck, seated on the sky-light, quietly smoking his cigar. I said, "General, are you not going to leave her?" "I don't believe she'll sink," he replied. "But she is an abandoned ship, sir; every one has left her." "Have they? are you sure?" "I'll make sure," I replied; and, going to the wheel-house, found it deserted. Then I looked into the engine-room—I remember the engine looked so grim and stiff in its solitude. Franklin then consented to go. We found a quiet place aft where there was no confusion; and as the waves tossed up our light vessel to a level with the steamer, he sprung upon her deck. As soon as he had jumped, I attempted to follow, but the vessel was not tossed high enough. So I watched my chance, and plunged head foremost into a port-hole, where friendly hands caught me, and prevented my falling on the deck.

But our little steamer would not sink. Franklin at once ordered out the boats, secured the captain and crew, and returned on board. We found that the outer shell of the boat was crushed in, and that she was leaking badly; but the inner ceiling was unhurt. We easily kept her free with the pumps until we had repaired damages. I do not think that the general ever quite forgave me for persuading him to leave her.

As we had failed by sea, we next tried the land, and with better success. We marched to Opelousas, driving the rebels before us. A pleasant incident happened on this march, one of those trifles which soften the horrors of war. I had known at New Orleans a charming rebel creole whose husband was a general in the Confederate army. I had had an opportunity to render the family some trifling service. One day we intercepted a courier bearing a letter from General —— to General Miles, commanding the district. He wrote that he had fallen upon the rear of our column and picked up a number of stragglers, and that he should send them next day to head-quarters. Of course we laid our plans, captured the escort, and recaptured our own men. With the general's assent, I sent the letter to the lady in question, with a line to the effect that she probably had not seen her husband's handwriting for some time, and might be gratified to learn from the inclosed letter that he was well. She would regret to learn, however, that our men had been retaken and the escort captured; that I should spare no pains to capture the general himself, and send him to his wife; and that if he knew what fate was in store for him, I was sure that he would make but a feeble resistance. She replied in the same spirit, that with such generous enemies war lost half its terrors.

Under Franklin nothing was left undone that

could properly be done to soften the rigors of war to non-combatants. Often have his staff officers spent weary hours over intercepted correspondence. It was our duty to examine the correspondence in search of intelligence that might be useful to us; but it was no part of our duty carefully to reseal those letters which were purely on domestic or personal matters, re-inclose the hundred odd little souvenirs they contained, and send them under a flag to the rebel lines. And yet we did this repeatedly. I wonder if the rebels ever did as much for us anywhere in the Confederacy!

Speaking of intercepted letters, I remember that at New Orleans we once seized a bag as it was about to cross the lake. Among other letters, it contained one from a young lady to her brother-in-law in Mobile. I have rarely seen a cleverer production. She gave an account, with great glee, of a trick she had played upon a Boston newspaper, perhaps the "Respectable Daily." She wrote that she had sent them a poem called "The Gypsy's Wassail," the original in Sanscrit, the translation of course in English, and all that was patriotic and loyal. "Now, the Sanscrit," she wrote, "was English written backward, and read as follows:

>   "'God bless our brave Confederates, Lord!
>   Lee, Johnson, Smith, and Beauregard!
>   Help Jackson, Smith, and Johnson Joe,
>   To give them fits in Dixie, oh!'"

The Boston newspaper fell into the trap, and published this "beautiful and patriotic poem, by our talented contributor." But in a few days some sharp fellow found out the trick and exposed it.

The letter was signed "Anna" simply, and no clue to the author was given. Anna thought that she was safe. She forgot that in the same bag was a letter from her sister to her husband, with signature and address, in which she said, "Anna writes you one of her amusing letters." So I had discovered who Miss Anna was, and wrote her accordingly. I told her that her letter had fallen into the hands of one of those "Yankee" officers whom she saw fit to abuse, and who was so pleased with its wit that he should take great pleasure in forwarding it to its destination; that in return he had only to ask that when the author of "The Gypsy's Wassail" favored the expectant world with another poem, he might be honored with an early copy. Anna must have been rather surprised.

As may be supposed, there were constant trials of

wit between the rebels and ourselves, in which we sometimes came off second best. But they had their women to help them, which gave them an immense advantage, for in such matters one woman is worth a "wilderness" of men. I recollect one day we sent a steamboat full of rebel officers, exchanged prisoners, into the Confederacy. They were generally accompanied by their wives and children. Our officers noticed the most extraordinary number of dolls on board—every child had a doll—but they had no suspicions. A lady told me afterward that every doll was filled with quinine. The sawdust was taken out and quinine substituted. Depend upon it that female wit devised that trick.

They attacked us in poetry too, generally written by young ladies, and some of it decidedly clever. Strong, Butler's adjutant-general, had stopped the service in one of the Episcopal churches, because the clergyman prayed for Jeff Davis instead of for the "President of the United States." This furnished a theme for some bitter stanzas. Banks had sent a light battery to drive among a crowd of women and children collected on the levee to see their friends off, and disperse them. This furnished a fruitful theme for the rebel muse.

To return to our Opelousas campaign.

We followed the course of the Teche for several days through a lovely country, the "Garden of Louisiana," and it deserves its name. The names in this part of the country are French. I remember we had a skirmish at a place called "Carrion-crow Bayou." It struck me as an odd name to give to a stream. I made inquiries, and found that a Frenchman had settled upon its banks, named Carran Cro.

Our march to Opelousas was without striking incident. The Confederates once or twice came into position, as if to dispute our progress, but they always gave way. Our return, however, was more eventful. The rebels attacked an outlying brigade, and caught it napping. It occupied a strong position, and could easily have beaten cavalry off, the only force by which it was attacked. Two regiments, however, were seized with a panic, and surrendered without firing a shot. The alarm was given to the main body, and re-enforcements quickly arrived, and drove off the rebels; but they carried off many prisoners. Not long afterward we turned the tables upon them. They encamped a regiment of Texas cavalry at a beautiful spot near Iberville, called

"Camp Pratt." Franklin organized an attack upon them. One night he sent our cavalry to make a wide détour upon the prairie and get into their rear. Then he attacked them in front with infantry. They mounted and fled in disorder, and fell, nearly to a man, into the hands of our cavalry. It was a well-organized and well-conducted expedition, and reflected credit upon Lee, who commanded the cavalry, and upon Cameron, who commanded the infantry. Tradition says that Dick Taylor, who commanded in that part of Louisiana, swore "like our army in Flanders" when he heard of it.

There is a very curious salt island near Iberville, well worth a visit, in a scientific point of view. Franklin wanted very much to explore it, but he did not wish to take an army as an escort, and he said it would be too absurd if he were captured on such an expedition. It would not have been quite so absurd for me, however; so I went, accompanied by Colonel Professor Owen, of the Indiana University, and volunteers, and with our head-quarters cavalry company as an escort. The island lies in the Gulf, and is perhaps half a mile in diameter. In the centre is a hollow about a hundred yards across, which has all the appearance of an extinct crater. Here, a few inches below the surface, lies the salt, in an almost perfect state of purity. For years our Southern brethren, who do not shine as inventors, sunk wells, pumped up the water, evaporated it, and so made their salt. At last it occurred to some one more clever than his neighbors, "Why not blast out the salt itself?" And so it was done. It seems scarcely possible, and yet I was credibly assured that so scarce was salt in the Confederacy, that wagons came all the way from Charleston, were loaded with salt, and returned to that city. It must have been a journey of months.

We wintered at Franklin, preparing for a spring campaign to the Red River. The climate of Louisiana is delicious in winter. I have tried both the South of France and Italy, but know no climate equal to that of Louisiana. The summer, *en revanche*, is intensely hot, and lasts from May to October, the thermometer ranging from 86° at night to 96° in the day-time. Yet the heat is not stifling. You feel no particular inconvenience from it at the time; but two seasons affect the nervous system seriously, and a white man must from time to time get the Northern or the sea-air. Happily the sea-coast is of easy access from New Orleans.

But while our command was under canvas, and

preparing for the approaching campaign, the cavalry was being mounted and drilled amidst the allurements of a large city. Why Banks did not send it to Thibodeaux, or to some other post where the prairie gave admirable opportunities for cavalry exercise, is a question which was often asked, but to which no satisfactory answer has ever been given. Farragut said that he feared that New Orleans would prove Banks's Capua. One of the consequences, as regards the cavalry, was, that they started upon the campaign with "impedimenta" enough for an army. Crossing a ford one day, Franklin spied a country cart drawn by a mule, containing bedding, trunks, and a negro woman. He sent the corps inspector to see to whom it belonged. It turned out to be the property of a sergeant of a cavalry regiment. Needless to say that the cart went no farther. After the rebels had captured their Champagne, sardines, and potted anchovies, at Sabine Cross Roads, they became excellent cavalry.

And now, fortunately for the navy, Bailey joined our staff. He had done such good work at Port Hudson—built half our works, got out a steamboat that lay high and dry in the mud, etc., etc.—that Banks had promoted him to be colonel of the regiment, over the head of the lieutenant-colonel. Banks had no right to do this. In so doing, he had usurped the prerogative of the Governor of Wisconsin; and the governor, as might be expected, resented it. Of course the governor was sustained by the War Department. Bailey was, naturally enough, annoyed and mortified, and wrote to me that he should leave the service; indeed, he supposed that he was already out of it, for he had been mustered out as major when he was mustered in as colonel; and now he had been mustered out as colonel. I wrote to him not to go off at half-cock, to write to the governor and ask in what capacity he recognized him, and then to the adjutant-general and ask the same question. He was answered by the governor that he recognized him as lieutenant-colonel, and by the Government that they recognized him still as major. He then wrote me that he would gladly remain in the service if I could get him on Franklin's staff, but that, under the circumstances, he could not return to his regiment. I spoke to the general upon the subject, and mentioned all that he had done under Sherman at Port Hudson and elsewhere. The general applied for him; he was ordered to report to us, and was announced as "Military Engineer of the Nineteenth Army Corps." Thus it happened that Bailey was with us when his regiment was not, and the fleet on the Red River consequently saved from destruction or capture.

CHAPTER VII.

Mistakes.—Affair at Mansfield.—Peach Hill.—Freaks of the Imagination.—After Peach Hill.—General William Dwight.—Retreat to Pleasant Hill.—Pleasant Hill.—General Dick Taylor.—Taylor and the King of Denmark.—An Incident.

I THINK it was on the 20th of March that we left for the Red River. We marched the whole distance, arriving at Natchitoches about the 3d of April. From Alexandria to Natchitoches we followed the Red River. Here began our mistakes. Banks arrived from New Orleans, and ordered us to take the inland road to Shreveport. Franklin suggested the river road, where the army and the fleet could render mutual support. Banks said no; that the other was the shorter route. It was the shorter in distance, but for the greater part of the way it was a narrow wood road, unfitted for the march of troops and the movement of artillery and wagons. We marched two or three days without interruption. Lee, who commanded the cavalry in advance, had often applied for a brigade of infantry to support him. Franklin had always declined to separate his infantry, answering that if Lee found the enemy too strong for him, to fall back, and we would come up with the whole infantry force and disperse them. On the evening of the 6th of April, I think it was, Banks came up at Pleasant Hill, and assumed command. The next day we were beaten; for that evening Lee again applied for his infantry, and got them. Franklin sent in a written remonstrance against the danger of separating the infantry, and having it beaten in detail. He was disregarded; and we marched to certain defeat.

The battle of Sabine Forks—Mansfield, the rebels call it; and as they won it, they have a right to name it—scarcely rises to the dignity of a battle. We had our cavalry and one brigade of infantry only engaged. We lost heavily, however, in guns and wagons, for the wagon-train of the cavalry followed close upon its heels, and blocked up the narrow road, so that the guns could not be got off. When Franklin heard from Banks that the cavalry and infantry brigade were seriously engaged, and that he must send re-enforcements, he at once ordered Emory up with the First Division of the Nineteenth Corps, and then rode forward himself to the scene of action. Here he lost his horse and was wounded in the leg, while one of our staff officers was killed. When our cavalry and brigade were finally defeated, the rebels advanced upon us. It was a striking and beautiful sight to see a column of their best infantry — the "Crescent City Regiment," I think it was — marching steadily down the road upon us, while their skirmishers swarmed through the woods and cotton fields. The column offered so beautiful a mark for a shell or two, that the general rode up to a retreating gun, and tried hard to get it into position, but the stampede was too general, and we had to look to our own safety. When he found how things were likely to turn out, Franklin had sent an aid-de-camp to Emory with orders to select a good position, come into line, and check the advancing enemy. Meantime, we retreated, abandoning the road—it was too blocked up—and taking to the woods and across the cotton fields, not knowing our whereabouts, or whether we should land in the rebel lines or in our own. At length we caught sight of Emory's red division flag, and a joyful sight it was. We soon reached it, and found that "Bold Emory" had chosen an excellent position on the summit of a gentle eminence, called

Peach Hill, and had already got his men into line. His division had behaved admirably. In face of cavalry and infantry retreating in disorder — and every officer knows how contagious is a panic — the First Division of the Nineteenth Army Corps steadily advanced, not a man falling out, fell into line, and quietly awaited the enemy. They did not keep us waiting long. In less than half an hour after we had joined the division, they appeared, marching steadily to the attack. But they were received with a fusillade they had not counted upon, and retreated in confusion. Again they attempted an attack on our right, but with no better success. They were definitively repulsed.

In this skirmish Franklin had another horse killed under him, shot in the shoulder, for the enemy's fire was very sharp for a few minutes. I offered him my horse, but he refused it. The captain of our head-quarters cavalry company offered him his, and he accepted it. The captain dismounted a private.

I saw here a striking instance of the effect produced by the imagination when exalted by the excitement of battle. A staff officer by my side dropped his bridle, threw up his arms, and said, "I am hit." I helped him from his horse. He said, "My boot is full of blood." We sent him to the ambulance. I said to myself, "Good-bye to —— I shall go to his funeral to-morrow." Next day he appeared at head-quarters as well as ever. He had been struck by a spent ball. It had broken the skin and drawn a few drops of blood, but inflicted no serious injury. At Port Hudson I saw the same effect produced by a spent ball. A man came limping off the field supported by two others. He said his leg was broken. The surgeon was rather surprised to find no hole in his stocking. Cutting it off, however, he found a black-and-blue mark on the leg—nothing more. The chaplain was reading to him, and the man was pale as death. I comforted him by telling him to send the stocking to his sweetheart as a trophy.

As we lay on our arms that night at Peach Hill without fire, for we were permitted to light none, lest we should reveal our small numbers to the enemy, we could hear distinctly the yells of the rebels as they found a fresh "cache" of the good things of the cavalry. It was very aggravating. They got our head-quarters ambulance too, but there was precious little in it. Expecting to bivouac, we had thrown a few things hastily into it. All they got of mine was a tooth-brush. I comforted myself with the reflection that they would not know what use to put it to.

Banks now sent for Franklin, and communicated to him his intention to remain on the battle-field all night, and renew the fight in the morning. Franklin represented that we had six thousand men at most, and the rebels thirteen thousand. Banks replied that A. J. Smith would be up. (Smith was thirteen miles in the rear, with eight thousand men.) "But how is he to get up, sir? The road is blocked up with the retreating troops and wagons, and is but a path, after all. He can't get up." "Oh! he'll be up—he'll be up;" and the interview ended. On his return to head-quarters, partly under a tree and partly on a rail fence, Franklin told me what had happened.

General William Dwight, of Boston, commanded the First Brigade of Emory's division. I knew Dwight well, for he had succeeded Sherman in command of our division at Port Hudson. I had recommended him highly to Franklin, when he was offered his choice of two or three generals for commands in the Nineteenth Corps, as an officer who could be thoroughly relied upon in an emergency. Dwight had said to me, "Major, if Franklin ever wants

Banks to do any thing, and he won't do it, do you come to me." I thought that the time had arrived to go to him; so I found my way through the darkness. "Well, general, we've got to stay here all night, and fight it out to-morrow." Dwight, who is quick as a flash, and whose own soldierly instinct told him what ought to be done, said at once, "Does Franklin think Banks ought to fall back upon A. J. Smith?" "Yes, he does." "Then I'll be d—d if he sha'n't do it. Wait here a minute." Dwight disappeared in the darkness. In ten minutes he returned and said, "It's all right; the order is given."

That night we fell back upon Pleasant Hill, Dwight bringing up the rear with his brigade. Franklin asked him if he could hold his position till half-past ten. "Till morning," he replied, "if you say so."

At Pleasant Hill we found General Smith with his "gorillas," as they were profanely called. Smith's command boasted that they had been in many a fight, and had never been defeated. I believe it was a true boast. It was partly luck, partly their own courage, and partly the skill with which they were handled. They were a rough lot, but good soldiers. I have seen them straggling along, one with a chicken hung to his bayonet, another with a pig on his back: turkeys, ducks, any thing of the kind came handy to them. The alarm sounded, and in an instant every man was in the ranks, silent, watchful, orderly, the very models of good soldiers.

The battle which now ensued at Pleasant Hill formed no exception to the rule which Smith's corps had established. The rebels, too, had been re-enforced, and attacked us in the afternoon with great spirit. But they soon found the difference between an affair with a single brigade of infantry, and one with three divisions fully prepared and admirably handled; for Franklin and Smith had made all the dispositions. They drove in the left of our first line, where we had a Five Points New York regiment (rowdies, by-the-way, always make the poorest troops); but they could make no impression on the second line, composed of Smith's "gorillas," and were beaten off with considerable loss.

General Dick Taylor, son of the President, commanded the rebel army in these engagements, and received much credit, and deservedly, for the manner in which he had defeated us at Mansfield. It was reported that General Smith, who commanded the Trans-Mississippi Department of the Confedcracy, found fault with Taylor for attacking us, as he had intended to draw us on to Shreveport, and there, with the help of Magruder from Texas, and Price from Arkansas, overwhelm us disastrously. Perhaps it was as well that we had it out at Mansfield. As regards the affair at Pleasant Hill, it was a mistake of the rebels. They were not strong enough to attack us in position. Taylor has since said that the attack was against his better judgment, but that the officers who had come up the night before wanted their share of glory. Perhaps, too, they had tasted the cavalry Champagne, and liked the brand. They might not have been quite so eager for the fray had they known what force they had to deal with at Mansfield, and what lay before them at Pleasant Hill.

The writer has since met General Taylor in London, and a most agreeable companion he is. He is a great favorite in court circles, largely for his own merits, but partly as "Prince Dick." In monarchical countries they can not divest themselves of the idea that our presidents are monarchs, and their children princes. "Prince John," "Prince Dick," "Prince Fred," all received quasi-royal honors. At Constantinople, when Fred Grant was with Sherman, a lieutenant on his staff, it was to Grant that the Sultan addressed his remarks. Grant tried to stop it, but could not.

They tell an amusing story of Dick Taylor in London. Taylor plays a good game of whist. The King of Denmark was on a visit to his daughter, and she sent for Taylor to make up a game with her father. Taylor won largely, and laughingly said to the king, "Your majesty can not find fault; I am only getting back those 'Sound Dues' my country paid Denmark for so many years."

Banks now wanted to continue his onward march to Shreveport, but A. J. Smith opposed it. He said that he belonged to Sherman's command, and had been lent to Banks for a season only; that he was under orders to return to Sherman by a certain day; that much time had been lost; and that if he undertook the march to Shreveport, he could not return by the date appointed. Our supplies, too, were rather short, the cavalry having lost their wagon-train. We fell back, therefore, upon Grand Ecore, where we rejoined the fleet. And here a curious incident occurred. An officer in high position came to Franklin and said that the army was in a very critical situation; that it required generalship to extricate it; that under Banks it would probably be captured or destroyed; and proposed to put Banks on board of a steamer, and send him to New Orleans, and that Franklin should take command. "And my men, general," he said, "will stand by you to the last man." Of course Franklin treated it as a joke, and laughed it off. But there can be no doubt that the officer was in earnest.

General Banks did not command the confidence of his troops, especially of the Western men. They generally spoke of him as "*Mr.* Banks." It was a great pity that his undoubted talent could not have been utilized in the civil service. As it turned out, he was perhaps the most striking instance in our service of the grave, almost fatal, mistake we made at the beginning of the war. He had been a good Speaker, so we made him a major-general; he had roused a certain interest in Massachusetts in her militia, so we gave him command of armies, and sent him out to meet trained soldiers like Stonewall Jackson and Dick Taylor. The result was a foregone conclusion.

CHAPTER VIII.

Low Water.—The Fleet in Danger.—We fall back upon Alexandria.—Things look Gloomy.—Bailey builds a Dam in ten Days.—Saves the Fleet.—A Skirmish.—Smith defeats Polignac.—Unpopularity of Foreign Officers.—A Novel Bridge.—Leave of Absence.—A Year in Virginia.—Am ordered again to New Orleans.

The Red River had now fallen very low. The gun-boats had great difficulty in descending the stream. One chilly evening, as we stood round the head-quarters camp-fire, word was brought us that one of Porter's best iron-clads was fast aground in the stream, and that they had tried in vain to get her off. I turned laughingly to Bailey, and said, "Bailey, can't you build a dam and get her off?" alluding to what he had done at Port Hudson. Bailey followed me to my tent and said, "Seriously, major, I think I *could* get that ship off, and I should like to try." I went immediately to the general, and got a letter from him to Porter, and sent Bailey to the grounded ship. She was built in compartments. He found them breaking in the partitions.

He remonstrated, and said, "Pump out one compartment, then shut it hermetically, and the confined air will help to buoy up the ship." The navy men, naturally enough, resented the interference of an outsider. Bailey gave Porter Franklin's letter. Porter said, "Well, major, if you can dam better than I can, you must be a good hand at it, for I have been d—g all night." Bailey had not met with a very encouraging reception. He was one of those serious men, who, as Sydney Smith said, require a surgical operation to get a joke into their heads. He returned to camp, and reported to me that Porter had insulted him. "What did he say, Bailey?" He told me; whereupon I explained to him the joke, and he was perfectly satisfied. "Oh, if that's what he meant, it's all right!" The ship was not got off. She was blown up and abandoned.

From Grand Ecore we fell back upon Alexandria. Franklin was put in command of the movement, and Bailey selected our line of march. We started at dark, and marched all night. But the Confederates were on the watch. They threatened our rear, and compelled us to halt, and deploy, while they hurried a strong force to take position at Kane's Ferry. Here we had a sharp skirmish. The position is a very strong one, the stream not being fordable at the Ferry. We crossed two brigades higher up. Moving slowly through the woods, for there were no roads, they struck the rebels on the left flank, and dislodged them. The fight was very sharp for a time. Colonel Fessenden, afterward brigadier-general, commanding a Maine regiment, and gallantly leading it, lost a leg in this affair.

But a severer trial awaited the fleet. About a mile above Alexandria the river shoots over a rapid, the Falls of Alexandria. On this shoal there was about five feet of water, and the river was falling. The boats drew from seven to nine feet. The floods come down with great rapidity in the Red River. One night's rain would have given the ships plenty of water. Twenty-four hours' hard rain raises it twenty feet. But the rain would not come. Things looked gloomy enough for the fleet. Bailey came to me and said that he could build a dam in ten days, and get those ships out. The river was six hundred and sixty-six feet wide at the Falls. Franklin sent me to Porter with the proposition. Porter said that it was not worth while — "It will rain to-night or to-morrow." To-night and to-morrow came, and it did not rain, and still the river fell.

Again Franklin sent me to Porter. I found him unwell and despondent. "Tell General Franklin," he said, "that if he will build a dam or any thing else, and get me out of this scrape, I'll be eternally grateful to him." I returned to Franklin. "Now go to Banks, and get his permission." I found Banks closeted with General Hunter. It was reported that the Government had become anxious about our command, and had sent Hunter down to examine and report upon our condition. I stated what was proposed. Banks turned to Hunter and said, "What do you think of it, general?" Hunter replied that he thought it impracticable, "But if Franklin recommends it, try it; for he is one of the best engineers in the army." Banks said, "Tell the general to give the necessary orders." The orders were given. Maine and Wisconsin regiments, principally lumbermen, were detailed for the work. In ten days the dam was built, the water rose, and the fleet came over in safety.

The rebels made a great mistake in not interfering with our work. Had they done so, they might have embarrassed us seriously on the left bank of the river, opposite Alexandria. But they never fired a shot. We were told that they laughed at the idea of damming the Red River, and said that we might as well try to dam the Mississippi. We would have done this, had it been necessary.

Bailey handled water as a lumberman handles his axe. One of the gun-boats was aground, hanging by the stern some little way above the Falls. They tugged at her with all sorts of mechanical contrivances, but in vain. In two hours Bailey built a little "wing-dam," he called it, turned the current under the stern of the vessel where she hung, washed out the sand, and the ship floated off.

Porter told me that if Bailey got his fleet out he would never rest till he was made a brigadier-general. He kept his word. The Government promoted him. The naval officers subscribed, and gave him a sword of honor and a service of plate. He deserved it all.

The fleet saved, we renewed our march to the Mississippi. It was made without incident, except that Smith defeated the rebels in a skirmish on the Atchafalaya. He practiced a ruse upon them: concealed a brigade in the deep dry ditches that intersect the sugar-fields there, then sent his skirmishers out. The rebs drove them in and pursued them; when up rose the men in the ditches, poured in a deadly fire, and took two hundred prisoners. We were not again troubled by the enemy.

Prince Polignac commanded the rebels upon this occasion. It was reported that he had come to Louisiana expecting that the Confederacy would become a monarchy; and it probably would have done so, had the Rebellion succeeded. I afterward heard that his defeat was not very disagreeable to his brother officers, for he was not popular with them. Indeed, very few foreign officers were popular on either side. Both Union and rebel officers were very much disposed to look upon it as a family quarrel, and wanted no interference from outsiders.

We crossed the Atchafalaya by a novel bridge constructed of steamboats. This, too, was Bailey's work. He anchored them side by side, the bows level with each other, and placed planks across them. The whole army, with its baggage-wagons and artillery, crossed safely and rapidly. A steam-whistle sounded, and in ten minutes the bridge had disappeared, and every boat was under full headway to its destination.

The writer's connection with the Department of the Gulf now ceased for a year. He obtained leave of absence, and went North. But he had scarcely arrived there when Early made his daring march upon Washington. My leave was revoked, and I was ordered to report to Major-general Gillmore. For a year I remained in Virginia, most of the time in Norfolk, for Gillmore had been thrown from his horse, and was unable to take the field in command of the Nineteenth Army Corps, as had been intended, and I had been assigned to a different duty. Early in the spring of 1865, on application of Brigadier-general T. W. Sherman, I was ordered again to New Orleans.

CHAPTER IX.

Visit to Grant's Head-quarters.—His Anecdotes of Army Life.—Banks relieved.—Canby in Command.—Bailey at Mobile.—Death of Bailey.—Canby as a Civil Governor.—Confiscated Property.—Proposes to rebuild Levees.—Is stopped by Sheridan.—Canby appeals.—Is sustained, but too late.—Levees destroyed by Floods.—Conflict of Jurisdiction.—Action of President Johnson.—Sheridan abolishes Canby's Provost Marshal's Department.—Canby asks to be recalled.—Is ordered to Washington.—To Galveston.—To Richmond.—To Charleston.—Is murdered by the Modocs.—His Character.

SHORTLY after my arrival at the North, I paid a visit of a few days to Colonel Badeau at Grant's head-quarters at City Point. Badeau had been with me on Sherman's staff. I staid at head-quarters in a tent reserved for guests, and messed with the general and his staff. Grant has the reputation of being a taciturn man, and he is generally so. But when seated on a summer's evening under the awning in front of his tent with his staff, and, perhaps, a few friends about him, he took his share of the conversation. He was full of anecdote, especially of army life. He talked very freely, not hesitating to express his opinions of men and things. Grant contended that no commanding officer could succeed in the long run, if he were not an honest and an honorable man. He did not care what were his talents, he was sure to come to grief, and injure the cause sooner or later. But Butler took different ground. He held that he could appoint clever and energetic officers to command, and benefit by their talents, while he could prevent their dishonesty from injuring the cause. Grant was undoubtedly right, and Butler wrong.

One evening, as we sat before his tent, Grant observed that he had that day sent orders to remove a certain general from high command in the West. I expressed my surprise, and said that I had always understood, and from army men too, that the officer in question was one of the best of our volunteer generals. Grant took his cigar from his mouth, and remarked, in his quiet way, "He's too much mixed up with cotton."

Politics makes strange bed-fellows. What a pity that President Grant was unable to carry into his civil appointments the same admirable principle upon which General Grant acted so inflexibly and so successfully in his military appointments! The officer whom he removed from command as "too much mixed up with cotton" he soon after appointed, under strong party pressure, to high civil office.

On my return to New Orleans, I found that Banks had been relieved, and Canby now commanded the Department of the Gulf. He was absent, engaged in the campaign against Mobile, which resulted in the capture of that city. Here Bailey again distinguished himself. The bay was strewed with torpedoes. Bailey had no fear of torpedoes. He told me that he had often navigated the Upper Mississippi when enormous cakes of ice, swept along by the rapid current, threatened to destroy the boat, but that it was easy enough by some mechanical contrivance to avoid them. He thought that torpedoes might be treated in the same way. He showed his faith by his works. He took the quartermaster's boats up without accident. The navy followed his lead, and safely. But the Admiral, changing his mind, ordered some of the boats back. In backing down, two were blown up and sunk.

But the war was now near its close. Bailey was shortly afterward mustered out of service, and returned to civil life. He removed from Wisconsin to Missouri, and settled in one of the border counties. Here he was elected sheriff. His end was a sad one.

With his usual daring, he attempted to arrest two noted desperadoes, horse-thieves, single-handed. They murdered him. He had not lived in vain. He had rendered good service to his country.

To return to Louisiana. The writer was now promoted to General Canby's staff, and became adjutant-general of the Department. Canby enjoyed the full confidence of the Government, and most justly. He had an exceedingly important command, extending from St. Louis to the Gulf, and from Florida to Texas. We had one hundred and eighty-seven thousand men upon our rolls. Canby was an excellent military commander, but his forte lay in civil government. Never was a Department better governed than was Louisiana in his day. A kind-hearted, benevolent gentleman, he gave one half of his pay to the rebel poor. Often have I seen his wife driving about New Orleans, accompanied by a Sister of Charity, dispensing his bounty. A clear-headed, just man, he governed that turbulent city with wisdom and justice, and with unflinching firmness. There were no riots in his day. More than once we were told that a riot was planned for the next day. Canby sent for Sherman; that night a battery would be quietly marched up from Jackson Barracks, and stationed out of sight in a cotton-press. Very early in the morning a company of cavalry picketed their horses in Esplanade Street. The quiet citizens saw nothing unusual, but the would-be rioters of course knew what had been done, and there was no riot. Canby was relieved; Sherman got leave of absence; and within a month a riot took place.

General Canby has saved millions of money to the United States. In these days of barefaced raids upon the Treasury, under color of bogus Southern claims, Canby's foresight and care are brought out in strong relief. When the war was ended, he returned all confiscated rebel property to its owners, but he took from them a release to the United States for all claim for rent or damage during our occupation. These men's mouths are now closed. The only exception he made was made most reluctantly under the orders of Sheridan. That great soldier does not shine in civil government as he does in the field. When he arrived in New Orleans, he told General Canby that he came there to take military command; that as for civil matters he knew nothing about them, and left them all to Canby. Before a month had passed an order came that General Canby would please report why he did not return the Metairie Ridge Race-course to its owners. This course was owned by gamblers. The gamblers of New Orleans are an institution and a power in that city. Canby replied with the indorsement, "Respectfully returned with a copy of the order bearing date (a month back) returning the Metairie Ridge Race-course to its owners on the usual conditions." The order came back, "General Canby will return the Metairie Ridge Race-course without condition." Canby felt deeply hurt. His carefully devised and impartially executed plan to protect the Treasury had been frustrated, and this in favor of a lot of gamblers. I do not doubt that these men are now before Congress as "loyal citizens," with their humble petition for reimbursement for the occupation of the race-course and the destruction of the fences.

Had Canby been permitted to have his own way, the levees in Louisiana would have been rebuilt in the fall of 1865, millions of money saved to the United States, and much suffering and vagabondage among the inhabitants avoided. In 1862 Butler had confiscated the crops on many abandoned estates. This property, when sold, realized a fund which was turned over to the successive Department commanders, to be used for various public purposes. Banks gave a monster concert, with artillery accompaniments, out of it, and balls, to dance the fair creoles into loyalty. Canby proposed to rebuild the levees. In his day the fund amounted to about eight hundred thousand dollars. He thought that this money, raised in Louisiana, could with propriety be expended in repairing the levees in Louisiana. He said expressly that the rebels had no right to this expenditure—as they had sown, so must they reap; but that it was in the interest of the United States and of humanity that he proposed to rebuild the levees. That if this were done, the people would be occupied, contented, and quiet, they would be no expense to the Government, and their crops would add to the general wealth of the country. That if it were not done, the plantations would be overflowed, the crops ruined, the inhabitants discontented, the value of the crops lost to the country, and the United States compelled, as a matter of humanity, to issue rations to the starving people. In the month of October, 1865, every thing was ready, the unemployed negroes enrolled, our negro regiments detailed, and the work about to commence, when it was stopped by an order from General Sheridan. Of course Sheridan did not do this from any mere caprice. He had his reasons, and to his mind they were conclusive. But they were purely technical and narrow. He said that the fund referred to did not belong to the Department; that it belonged to the Treasury, or at least to the Quartermaster-general, and could not be used without his assent. Canby was always most reluctant to appeal from his superior officer to higher authority, but he thought that in this instance the interests of his Department, and those of the United States itself, were too deeply involved for him to accept Sheridan's decision. He appealed to Washington, and was sustained. But the Government, instead of ordering him to commence the work at once, sent out a board of engineers—Barnard at the head—to survey the levees, and agree upon plans for repairing them. At length all these most unnecessary formalities were got through with, and Canby was ordered to proceed with the work. This was promptly done. But it was now January, instead of October. In February the water rose, and swept away all that had been done. All the evils predicted by Canby now came upon the country. And not for that year only, but for several succeeding years, the Government was compelled to feed a suffering, discontented, and turbulent population.

Several nice and novel legal questions arose on the termination of the war in reference to confiscated property. These were determined by General Canby so wisely and so justly that the Quartermaster-general not unfrequently sent to him for copies of his orders as guides for the Department at Washington in its own decisions. I recollect one question particularly, which brought him into conflict with the United States District Judge. It will be remembered that at the close of the war an immense quantity of cotton was found stored in the by-ways of the Confederacy, especially far up the Red River. Part of this cotton was undoubtedly liable to confiscation, but the greater part was not. Treasury agents thronged all over the South. The character of these men "left much to be desired," as the Frenchman politely puts it. They were "on the make." Their object was to prove all cotton liable to confiscation, for the law gave them a large percentage of the proceeds. The amount of perjury committed by these men, and by the professional perjurers whom they employed, was fearful. The effect was demoralizing to the last degree, and exasperated the inhabitants; while it was the object of the Government, and the earnest desire of the victorious North, to pacify the

South by dealing not only justly, but generously, by it. Canby felt this, and with his usual sagacity and foresight made a proposition to the Secretary of the Treasury, which, if adopted, would have saved the Government millions in money, and more than millions in peace and good-will. He proposed that ports should be designated on the Mississippi for the receipt of cotton; that every pound arriving there should pay the Government twenty-five cents, or fifty cents (any thing that the Government might designate), and that no questions should be asked as to its origin. Mr. M'Culloch replied that it was an admirable plan, but that there were reasons why it could not be adopted. The reason, I fear, was the influence brought to bear at Washington by the nascent race of carpet-baggers. There was money in the Treasury-agent system.

This system led, as I have said, to a collision between the military and the judicial authorities in New Orleans, which in any other hands than Canby's might have been serious. M'Culloch wrote to the general asking him to sustain his agents with the military power in their seizure of cotton. Canby of course replied that he would do so. Shortly afterward an agent applied to us for a military force.

He had seized a lot of cotton, and brought it to New Orleans. The owner, an alleged Union man, had applied to the United States District Court, and the United States Marshal had been ordered to take possession of it. He attempted to do so, but was, of course, repulsed by the military, the city being still under martial law. The judge thereupon issued an order for Canby to appear before him, and show cause why he held the cotton against the process of the court. The order was an impertinent one; for the judge knew well enough that the city was still under martial law. The judge was that Durell who afterward came to grief. But Canby always showed the greatest respect to the judiciary. I remember, as if it were yesterday, seeing him start for the court-room at the appointed time, in full uniform, accompanied by Major De Witt Clinton, his judge-advocate. His return to the order of the court was to my mind conclusive. He said, substantially, that the United States District Court was a creation of the law; that it possessed precisely those powers which had been conferred upon it by Congress, and no others; that if this cotton had been captured by the navy on the high seas, he should have surrendered it at once on the order of the judge, for the court was clothed with admiralty jurisdiction, but that it had no military jurisdiction, and that he had no right to surrender, and might be held responsible for surrendering, powers which, under martial law, were vested in him alone. The judge reserved his decision. The claimant's lawyers telegraphed to the President; and Johnson, who was then beginning to coquet with the Democrats, contrary to Stanton's advice, and without waiting for Canby's report, ordered the cotton to be given up, to the general's great satisfaction; for it soiled the fingers of every one who touched it.

General Canby had now been thwarted twice by General Sheridan in purely civil matters — matters belonging properly to the commander of the Department. He felt as if his usefulness were gone, and prepared a letter to the Adjutant-general asking to be relieved from his command, and ordered elsewhere. He showed me this letter. I felt that his loss to the Department would be irreparable, and I persuaded him to withhold it. But shortly afterward Sheridan again interfered with the civil government of the city, and this time by breaking up the provost-marshal's department of General Canby's own staff. It is a matter of great delicacy for one general to interfere with the staff of another. Canby felt deeply hurt, and told me that he should forward his letter to Washington. Of course I could no longer object; for it seemed to me that self-respect left him no choice. He was relieved at once, for he was all-powerful with Stanton, who had the highest esteem and regard for him, and unbounded confidence in his integrity and wisdom. He was made president of a most important board on war claims, sitting at Washington. But shortly afterward there was disturbance in Texas, and Canby was immediately sent there. Again, there was disturbance in Virginia, and Canby was transferred to Richmond. Then came difficulty in South Carolina, and at once Canby was ordered to Charleston. Wherever he went, order and tranquillity followed his footsteps.

This wise, great, and good man lost his life miserably. He fell a victim to the Peace Commission. He commanded the Department in which Captain Jack and those wretched Modocs gave us so much trouble. Although the force operating against the Indians numbered but five hundred men, and the weather was so severe that the ink froze in his tent, Canby thought it his duty to go in person to the

"Lava Beds." Here he was rapidly unearthing the savages from "their caves and dens in the rocks," when the Peace Commission begged him to send the Indians a flag of truce and invite them to a "talk." He replied that it was useless; that he knew the Indians far better than those gentlemen could; and that the best and most humane method was to follow up his military advantages. They entreated, and appealed to his love of peace. He yielded, went unarmed and without escort to the conference, and was murdered by the savages. Thus died one of the best, ablest, and purest men the war had brought to the front.

The writer left Louisiana in June, 1866, and shortly afterward, on his own request, was mustered out of the service. He looks back with pleasure to the years passed in that lovely and fruitful land. He regrets the evil days which have fallen upon it, and can not but think that the upright and honorable men whom he knew there—and there are plenty of them among its inhabitants—must regret the loss of the rule of justice, law, order, and economy under Canby, when they contrast it with the infamous rule of the carpet-baggers—fraud and corruption on one side met by violence and intimidation on the other.

CHAPTER X.

The Writer appointed Assistant Secretary of Legation to Paris.—Presented to the Emperor.—Court Balls.—Diplomatic Dress.—Opening of Corps Législatif.—Opening of Parliament.—King of the Belgians.—Emperor of Austria.—King of Prussia.—Queen Augusta.—Emperor Alexander.—Attempt to assassinate him.—Ball at Russian Embassy.—Resignation of General Dix.

In October, 1866, at the request of General Canby, Mr. Seward appointed the writer to be Assistant Secretary of Legation at Paris. Johnson was then President, but he very properly left all these minor appointments in the State Department to its chief. Frederic Seward told me that it was impossible to have a better friend at their court than General Canby—"they always accepted his bills at sight."

General Dix had then been named Minister to France, but had not sailed. Mr. Bigelow still filled the office. On presenting my credentials, he requested me to await the arrival of the General before entering upon my duties, that the proposed changes might all be made at the same time.

Late in December General Dix arrived, and was

presented. Court carriages were sent for the minister, and he was accompanied by the secretaries of legation, and by the "Introducteur des Ambassadeurs" in gorgeous uniform. Those were the halcyon days of the diplomatic service, before Congress had come to the conclusion that the safety of the republic depended upon its foreign representatives being dressed in swallow-tail coats. We were then permitted to dress like other gentlemen of the diplomatic corps in the same grade.

The Emperor was always happy in his reception of the diplomates accredited to him. The custom was to send in advance to the Minister of Foreign Affairs a copy of the address to be delivered, that the Emperor's reply might be prepared. These speeches, under ordinary circumstances, might be stereotyped: change the names, and one will answer for another. After the formal addresses, an informal conversation followed. General Dix then presented the secretaries. The Emperor spoke English very well, and liked to ventilate it. He did not speak it perfectly, however, as was claimed by his enthusiastic admirers. He translated French into English, as we so often translate English into French. He said, for instance, to Colonel Hay, "You have made *ze* war in *ze* United States?" ("*Vous avez fait la guerre?*") meaning, "Did you serve?" Hay was strongly tempted to tell him that it was not he; it was Jeff Davis.

After the presentation to the Emperor, we paid our respects to the Empress. That charming and beautiful woman was then in the zenith of her beauty and grace. She received us in her bonnet and walking-dress, as she had come from mass; for in Catholic countries diplomatic presentations generally take place on Sunday. Nor in Catholic countries only, for in England the Prince of Wales sometimes receives on that day. The Empress too speaks English, and with less accent than the Emperor, though not so fluently.

The imperial court in 1866–'67 was at the height of its splendor. France was apparently prosperous and powerful, and Paris reigned the queen-city of the world. All nations paid her willing tribute. She was preparing for the Exhibition of 1867, the most successful ever held, except our own at Philadelphia. The winter was unusually gay, the palace setting the example. As a rule, the Emperor gave four grand balls during the season. They were very magnificent, and would have been very pleasant except for the great crowd. But those balls were given principally to the military, and the garrison of Paris thronged them to the number of two or three thousand. Some of the subordinate officers were wholly unused to any other society than that of the barracks, and they brought their barrack manners with them, crowding, pushing, treading upon the ladies' dresses, scratching their shoulders with their epaulets. When the supper-room was opened, the Centgarde on duty at the door had great difficulty in keeping back the hungry crowd. Once they actually broke through and rushed in. The sentries were thereupon doubled, but even then were compelled to threaten to report the most prominent disturbers to the Emperor. Every private in the Centgardes ranked as an officer of the army.

It may interest some of my readers to know how presentations were made at these balls. The United States Minister was allowed to present twenty-six persons in all. They were selected generally upon the principle of first come, first served; but the matter rested wholly in his discretion. No one had a right to a presentation. Mr. Seward settled this in a clear and positive dispatch to Mr. Dayton, and his instructions now regulate the action of our ministers in most of the courts of Europe. Occasionally we asked for one or two extra presentations. The inquiry was then generally made, "Is it a young and pretty woman?" If it were, there was no difficulty, for the Empress, like other ladies, was pleased to have her balls set off with beautiful and well-dressed women. American ladies were always well received by her for this reason. Her balls were sometimes called by the envious "*bals américains.*"

The persons to be presented were arranged round one of the rooms at the Tuileries. The Emperor entered and passed down the line, each person being named to him. He sometimes stopped, though rarely, and addressed a few words to one of the presentees. The Empress followed in the same manner. She exacted that every lady should be in full evening dress, and if by chance one slipped in not *décolletée*, the minister was pretty sure to hear of it. General Dix was once asked to present a young lady with her mother. He consented. She turned out to be a child of fourteen. Before many days he heard that the Empress had said that she did not receive children.

But the Empress's Mondays, *petits lundis*, were charming. They were not unpleasantly crowded, and they were composed exclusively of people who knew how to behave themselves. Frequently they were musical parties, and there one heard the best musical talent of the world. No money was paid to the leading artists; for the theory is that the honor of singing before the sovereign is sufficient; but a bracelet or other piece of jewelry was sent to the singer, and always of value, for the Emperor was very generous — too much so for his own interests and those of his family, as events have shown.

The *petits lundis* were a paradise for our American diplomates. There we wore our swallow-tail coats, with black tights and silk stockings. The most rabid anti-uniformist could not object to that. To wear swallow-tail at one of the balls, however, was by no means a pleasant duty. After one or two experiments our secretaries gave up going. The French officers—not those of high rank, of course—would stare with all the impertinence they could muster, and take the opportunity to jostle them accidentally in the crowd. It was very different in London. If one of us went to a ball at Buckingham Palace in mufti, the page at the door simply asked, "United States, sir?" and he passed in without difficulty. Of course every one present noticed the dress, but no one appeared to do so. They evidently felt sorry for the poor devil who found himself in such an awkward fix, and wished to make it as easy for him as possible. French politeness did not shine by the contrast.

Early in the winter the Emperor opened the Corps Législatif. In all constitutional monarchies this is an occasion of great ceremony and splendor. A hall in the Louvre was used for the purpose. All the great bodies of state attended in their gorgeous uniforms. Senators, deputies, judges, members of the Academy and of the Institute, marshals, admirals —every thing that France possessed of glorious in arms, or eminent in literature, science, art, and statesmanship, was congregated there. When all was ready, the Empress, attended by the ladies of the imperial family, and by her ladies in waiting, walked up the whole length of the centre aisle to her seat on the throne, amidst the indescribable enthusiasm of the audience. Her beauty, her grace, and her stately bearing carried the enthusiasm to its height. You would have sworn that every man there was ready to die for his sovereign. Within less than four years she sought in vain for one of them to stand by her in her hour of danger.

The opening of the Corps Législatif, splendid and

interesting as it was, did not compare in either respect—in American eyes, at least—with the opening of Parliament by the Queen in person. She has done this so rarely of late that, when she does appear, the interest and excitement in London are very great. The ceremony takes place in the House of Lords. The peers are in their robes of office, scarlet and ermine. Each particular robe is ugly enough, very much like red flannel and cat-skin; but the effect of all together is very fine. The peeresses are in full dress. The diplomatic corps are present in their rich uniforms. The princes enter and take their seats as lords. That graceful and beautiful woman, the Princess of Wales—perhaps the most beautiful woman in England—and the Princess Mary and the Duchess of Edinburgh, follow and take their seats upon the wool-sack facing the throne. When all is ready, the Queen, preceded by the white rod and the black rod (they call them the "sticks" in England), the lord chancellor and the lord chamberlain, and all her high officers of state, appears and seats herself upon the throne, the Princess Louise and the Princess Beatrice supporting her on either side. Short and stout as is the Queen, she has the most graceful and stately walk perhaps in Europe. It is a treat to see her move. Then the lower doors are opened; there is a rush and a scramble, and loud voices are heard, and the Commons of England, headed by their Speaker, the very body for whom all this show and state and splendor are got up, crowd into a narrow space behind a railing, and there stand while the Queen reads her speech. It seems strange, when one reflects that the Commons really govern England, to see them shut out in the cold as if they were not fit to associate with the distinguished company present. When the speech is finished, the Speaker bows, the Queen descends from the throne, the Commons return to their House, and the pageant is ended.

The Great Exhibition opened on the 1st of May, 1867. It was not nearly ready, but was opened punctually to the day with all the well-arranged ceremony for which the French are noted. The sovereigns of Europe began to flock to Paris. "The Grand Duchess of Gerolstein" was then in the full tide of success at one of the theatres. It was odd to note that among the first visits the great royalties paid (the Emperor of Russia and the King of Prussia) was one to "The Grand Duchess." The minor sovereigns, the kinglings, rarely went;

and when they did, they saw nothing amusing in it.

The diplomatic corps had admirable opportunities to see the different sovereigns visiting Paris. It is the custom for a monarch to receive the diplomatic corps accredited to the capital at which he is a guest. We stood in a circle, and, while the royal visitor talked to our own minister and to those near him on either side, we had excellent opportunities to study his features, expression, and manners. The most agreeable of them all, with an apt word for every one, was the King of the Belgians. He had a great deal to say to General Dix about Mr. Seward, whom he had known, and the port of Antwerp as convenient for American shipping. He spoke English admirably. He was accompanied by the Queen, a young and pretty woman, who, by-the-way, was the only sovereign lady who came to the Exposition, much to the Empress's disappointment, and somewhat, it was said, to her mortification. Next in tact to the King of the Belgians came the Emperor of Austria, a small, well-made, military-looking man, with most polished manners. He spoke to me—for General Dix was then temporarily absent—of his brother, the Emperor Maximilian, and expressed his gratitude to our Government for its efforts to save his life. Later, while *chargé* at London, I met the Empress of Germany. She, too, has the gift of saying the right thing in the right place. I heard her conversation with two or three of my colleagues who stood near me. It was always happy. To me she spoke of all that the Legation at Paris had done to protect "*mes pauvres Allemands dans ces tristes, ces pénibles circonstances.*" She was glad to have the opportunity to thank me in person, and wished me to convey her thanks to Mr. Washburne.

But the chief guest, the man to whom all eyes were turned, was the Emperor of Russia, a pale, handsome, silent, gentlemanly-looking man. For him reviews were held, gala operas given, and magnificent fêtes at the Tuileries and at the Hôtel de Ville. I doubt if the world ever saw a more beautiful fête than that given to him by the Empress at the Tuileries. It was summer, the month of June. The gardens of the palace were closed to the public. The flower-beds (the flowers were then in full bloom) were bordered with gas-jets, the trees were festooned with variegated lamps, the fountains played, and electric lights—blue, pink, and yellow—were thrown alternately upon the sparkling waters. It was very beautiful. And when, at midnight, the Empress, accompanied by a number of ladies, and by the Emperors and their suites, descended into the gardens, and the electric light flashed on their bright dresses and jewels, and brilliant uniforms, the effect was fairy-like.

The review was next in order. Sixty thousand men passed before the Emperors without check or delay. The King of Prussia was present, accompanied by Bismarck and Moltke. Bismarck even then attracted much attention. I have rarely seen a finer-looking man. More than six feet high, large and powerful in proportion, with a grand head well set upon the shoulders, he looks like Agamemnon—"king of men."

It was on the return from this review that the Emperor of Russia was shot at by a Pole. Fortunately, he was not hit. The only creature hurt was the horse of one of the equerries. The blood spurted from a wound in the animal's neck upon the Emperor's second son, who was in the carriage with him. The father's only thought was for his son; and, leaning forward, he laid his hand tenderly upon him while he anxiously inquired if he was wounded. It was reported that the Emperor of the French turned to his imperial guest, and said, "Sire, we have been under fire together for the first time to-day;" to which the Emperor replied, with much solemnity of manner, "Sire, we are in the hands of Providence."

That evening I saw him at a ball at the Russian embassy. It was very small, not more than two hundred persons present. He looked pale and *distrait*, evidently anticipating, with some apprehension, the effect to be produced in Russia, and upon her relations with France, when the news should reach St. Petersburg. Madame Haussmann, the wife of the Prefect of the Seine, a well-meaning woman, but who did not shine precisely by her tact, was trying to make conversation with him. He looked over her head, as if he did not see her, and finally turned upon his heel and left her. It was not perhaps polite, but it was very natural. The Emperor and Empress of the French made extraordinary exertions to enliven the ball, but there was a perceptible oppression in the air. The would-be assassin was not condemned to death. Strange to say, a French jury found "extenuating circumstances." But the French sympathize strongly with the Poles; and I doubt if, under any circumstances, a French jury would condemn to death a Pole who had attempted to murder a Russian.

The Emperor of Russia is a man of the highest sense of personal honor. When lately he sought an interview with the English embassador, and assured him on his honor that he had no thought of conquest, or any desire to occupy Constantinople, those who know his character believed him implicitly. It was reserved for certain ultra Tory journals in London to doubt his word. No language would be strong enough for these journals to employ if a Russian newspaper were to doubt the word of honor of Lord Derby or any other prominent English gentleman. Happily, the *Standard* and its *confrères* do not yet direct public opinion in England.

In the fall of 1867, the Exhibition closed with great ceremony, and Paris settled down for a time to the even tenor of its way. In 1868, General Grant was elected President, and was inaugurated in 1869. In the spring of this year General Dix resigned. He preferred the comforts of his home, with the society of his children and grandchildren, to the attractions of the imperial court. No minister ever represented the United States with more dignity than General Dix. A man of marked ability, an accomplished scholar and gentleman, he possessed precisely those qualities which are the most highly prized at a court like that of France. The ladies, too, of his family shone in their sphere; a matter of much greater importance than is generally supposed in our country. The general has left a very pleasant impression in France; and not unfrequently since the fall of the empire I have been stopped in the street by some sad looking ex-official with inquiries after his health.

CHAPTER XI.

Washburne appointed Minister.—Declaration of War.—Thiers opposes it.—The United States asked to protect Germans in France.—Fish's Instructions.—Assent of French Government given.—Paris in War-paint.—The Emperor opposed to War.—Not a Free Agent.—His *Entourage*.—Marshal Le Bœuf.

In the month of May, 1869, Mr. Washburne arrived in France, and entered upon the duties of his office. In the mean time I had been promoted, at the request of General Dix, to be secretary of legation. At Mr. Washburne's request, I was retained in that position. Paris was uneasy and restless. Conspiracies against the empire were rife. The Republicans, as they called themselves—Radicals is a better name for the majority of them—became bold and defiant. France was jealous, too, of the renown acquired by Prussia at Sadowa. She had been so accustomed to consider herself, and to be considered, the first military power in the world, that she could not bear the semblance of a rival near the throne. The Emperor was suffering from the disease of which he afterward died, and no longer governed with "the hand of steel in the glove of silk" always needed in France. The Church was alarmed at the rise of a great Protestant power, and the Empress sympathized with her Church. In short, public sentiment had reached such a pass in France, or rather in Paris, which is France, that the Emperor was compelled to choose between war and revolution. He naturally chose war. It was definitely resolved upon on the 15th July, 1870, but not officially declared until the 19th. I was *chargé d'affaires*, Mr. Washburne being absent at Carlsbad.

On the 13th of July I went to the sitting of the Corps Législatif to learn what were the prospects of war. In the tribune of the diplomatic corps I met the Spanish Embassador. He told me that peace was assured, as he had persuaded Prince Hohenzollern to decline the proffered crown of Spain, and that now nothing remained to fight about. On the 14th, I went again. I found Lord Lyons there, and, falling into conversation with him, he left the impression upon my mind that there would be war, for the proffered mediation of England had failed. Lord Lyons had come to the sitting expecting to hear an authoritative declaration by the Government, and this declaration he thought would be warlike. I at once telegraphed to Mr. Fish that the chances were strongly in favor of war. This, and all our subsequent telegrams in cipher, were delayed by the French Government for twenty-four hours, probably with a view to decipher them. On the 15th I was again at the *séance*, and heard the warlike declaration made by the Government. It was not the formal declaration of war, but was equivalent to it. Thereupon Mr. Thiers rose, and attempted to address the House in a speech deprecating hostilities. The scene that followed was indescribable and most disgraceful to any legislative body. The great mass of the members sprung to their feet, pointed their fingers at the orator, yelled, and shouted "*Traître, traître! Allez à Berlin!*" The little man stood like a rock, and when the tumult had somewhat subsided, I could hear his shrill, piping voice raised in solemn warning against the step they were about to take. The Government had stated that their embassador had been insulted by the King of Prussia. Mr. Thiers asked that the dispatches might be produced, that the Assembly might judge for itself. This the Government refused; and, on a show of hands, but twenty members—among whom were Favre, Arago, Simon, Pelletan, and others, most of them afterward prominent in the Government of the National Defense—voted with Thiers.

While the debate was proceeding I was called out by the messenger of the Legation, with word that the German Embassador was very anxious to see me. As soon as the proceedings in the Corps Législatif were ended, I went to the German embassy. The embassador told me that he had been instructed by his Government to ask the United States Legation at Paris to assume the protection of the North Germans in France during the coming war. I saw at once the importance of this step, the compliment paid us by a great power like Germany, and the advantages to the country. I replied that I felt confident that my Government would gladly assume the charge; that if there were no cable across the Atlantic, and it were necessary to say "Yes" or "No" at once, I should say "Yes;" but as there was telegraphic communication, and I could receive an answer in forty-eight hours, I must ask instructions from Mr. Fish. He appeared to be disappointed, and inquired when I could give him an answer, as he must leave Paris in two days. He evidently desired the matter to be settled before he left. I told him that I thought I should receive a reply within that time.

I went at once to the office, and telegraphed Mr. Fish as follows. This telegram, like the other, was detained for twenty-four hours by the French Government.

"Paris, July 15th, 1870.

"Fish — *Washington:*—War is certain. Can I take Prussian subjects in France under our protection? Have promised answer to-morrow.

"Hoffman."

On the 17th I received Mr. Fish's answer, as follows:

"Washington, July 16th, 1870.

"Protection of North Germans in French territory by American representative can only be given at request of North Germany, and with assent of France. Examine request of Mr. Moustier of July 16th, 1867, to United States to protect French in Mexico. Fish."

On receipt of this instruction, I wrote at once to the Duke de Gramont, to ask for the assent of the French Government. My note was as follows:

"Legation of the United States,
Paris, July 17th, 1870.

"Sir,—I was requested by the embassador of the North German Confederation, before his departure from Paris, to take the North German subjects residing on French territory under the protection of this Legation. To-day I am in receipt of a telegram from my Government authorizing me to do so, provided that it be done with the assent of his majesty's Government. I have the honor to apply for this assent.

"I have the honor, etc., etc., etc.,
"WICKHAM HOFFMAN.

"His Excellency the DUKE DE GRAMONT,
Etc., etc., etc."

The Duke de Gramont replied, on the 18th, that the French Government gave its "entire assent," whereupon I telegraphed to Mr. Fish as follows:

"FISH — *Washington :*—Consented to take North Germans under protection on application of embassador, and with assent of France. * * * * Washburne returns immediately.   HOFFMAN."

I learned afterward that my note to the Duke de Gramont produced quite a sensation in the Emperor's cabinet. The French Government had already requested the good offices of Great Britain to protect French subjects in North Germany, and it had fully expected that North Germany would make a similar request. Speculation was therefore rife in official circles as to what the action of Count Bismarck meant. It was supposed that he anticipated a general European war, into which Great Britain would necessarily be drawn; and preferred, therefore, to ask the good offices of a power which under all circumstances was likely to remain neutral.

The Duke de Gramont was then Minister of Foreign Affairs, and was supposed to have had much to do with bringing on the war. The story was current in Paris that, when he was embassador at Vienna, Bismarck represented Prussia. They quarreled, and Bismarck remarked of him, "*C'est l'homme le plus bête d'Europe.*" He never forgave it. At Vienna he naturally associated with the Viennese aristocracy, who disliked the Prussians. From them he got the idea that Austria would readily join France in a war against Prussia, and so reported to the Emperor. He took no note of the all-powerful middle class, which rules in constitutional countries. This class would not hear of becoming allies of France in a war against Germany.

Late in the evening of the 18th of July, Mr. Washburne returned to Paris. He had been at Carlsbad for his health, but on learning the probability of hostilities, started at once on his return to his post. We had telegraphed him, but he never received the telegram. Few private telegrams were forwarded at all, and none with promptitude, in those days.

Paris now put on its war-paint. The streets were gay with the *pantalon rouge*, and all day long the French drum rat-a-tapped in the streets. The Mobiles began to arrive, the National Guard to parade —everywhere was heard the "Marseillaise." The forbidden air was delightful to Parisian ears, because it was forbidden. Long before the end of the siege it was rarely heard. The Parisians could chant it as they pleased, so it soon lost its attractions.

The war was popular in Paris. The journals clamored for it, and the violent republican papers, whatever they may now say to the contrary, were among the most blatant. The Emperor, personally, was opposed to war. He was suffering from the acute disease which afterward killed him, and was naturally depressed and despondent. He would gladly have avoided hostilities, but he was pushed into them. They persuaded him, too, that the continuance of his dynasty, the succession of his son, demanded war; and this was the one ruling motive which governed both his conduct and that of the Empress. The Emperor was by no means the omnipotent potentate he was popularly supposed to be.

He was scarcely a free agent. It was his misfortune to be surrounded by a crowd of adventurers—French carpet-baggers. The best men of France, the gentry of the country, held aloof. The Emperor felt this, and often tried to reconcile them. Had he reigned ten years longer, I think that he would have succeeded. There were signs of relenting. He was consequently thrown, for his high officers of state, upon a class of clever adventurers. Look at his last cabinet before the Revolution of September. One member was most unenviably known for the loot of the Summer Palace at Pekin; another is now in Mazas, convicted of swindling; and a third, it was currently reported in Paris, received one hundred thousand francs in the Transcontinental, Memphis, and El Paso swindle; and I have heard from high Prussian authority that when the gates of Paris were opened after the siege, and the Germans sold flour and cattle and sheep to meet the pressing necessities of the starving Parisians, of a flock of three thousand sheep not one was permitted to enter the city till this gentleman had received two francs a head.

I have said that the Emperor was scarcely a free agent. Here is an anecdote in point. Prince Metternich, the Austrian Embassador, returning from Vienna, called to pay his respects at the palace. The Emperor asked him what military news there was in Austria. He replied that they were arming with the Remington breech-loader. "The Remington," said the Emperor, "what is that? I thought I knew all the principal breech-loaders, but I never heard of that." Metternich explained. "Where is Remington?" said the Emperor. The Prince replied that he happened to be in Paris. "I wish you would bring him to me, and do you bring him yourself; this will insure my seeing him." Metternich brought him. The Emperor examined his piece, and was much pleased with it. He wrote a note with his own hand to the Minister of War, Le Bœuf, and told Remington to take it at once: of course he was received without delay. "So, my good friend, you have seen the Emperor, have you?" "Yes, sir, I had the honor to see his Majesty." "Well, you won't see him again:" and he did not. This was the way the Emperor was served. Le Bœuf was the capable and well-informed Minister of War who stated in the Assembly that France was thoroughly prepared for the field—"not a button on a gaiter was wanting." When the sad truth became known, the French wits said that his statement was literally correct, for there was not a gaiter in store.

But while the war was popular in Paris, it was not so in the provinces. After the Revolution broke out, the Provisional Government found in the Tuileries a number of important historical documents, and among them reports from the prefects of the different departments on this subject. They breathed one tone. The people wanted peace; but if they were attacked, if the honor of France were at stake, they were ready to fight. Considering the source whence this information came, from imperial prefects, creatures of the Government, there was no mistaking the pacific feeling of the country.

CHAPTER XII.

Germans forbidden to leave Paris.—Afterward expelled.—Large Number in Paris.—Americans in Europe.—Emperor's Staff an Incumbrance.—French Generals.—Their Rivalries.—False News from the Front.—Effect in Paris.—Reaction.—Expulsion of Germans.—Sad Scenes.—Washburne's Action.—Diplomatic Service.—Battle of Sedan.—Sheridan at Sedan.

And now began our labors at the Legation, increasing from day to day, until we had thirteen distinct nationalities under our charge, European and South American. Nor was this all. The citizens of other countries—countries which had not formally asked our protection—came to us for assistance. This was particularly the case with Mexico and Roumania. There was a large colony of Mexicans in Paris, and Mexico had no representative in France. The diplomatic relations which were suspended by the Mexican war are still unrenewed, notwithstanding the friendly efforts of our Government. As regards Roumania, its position is peculiar. Nominally it is under the suzerainty of Turkey, and the Turk claims to represent it abroad. But Roumania does not ac-

7

quiesce in this claim, and appoints its own agents, who are quasi-recognized by the powers to whom they are accredited. There was a large number of Roumanian students in Paris at the outbreak of the war. These young men were left quite destitute during the siege. The French Government behaved very generously by them. At Mr. Washburne's suggestion, it made them a monthly allowance, sufficient for their support.

The French Government had at first decided that no German should leave France to return home. The reason given for this harsh measure was that every German was a soldier, and would go to swell the enemy's ranks. It was very hard on the Germans in France. They were thrown out of employment, insulted, liable to violence, and sometimes assaulted, and, in addition to all this, were treated as *insoumis* at home, and subject to severe punishment for neglect of military duty. Mr. Washburne remonstrated against this measure, and wrote an able dispatch to the Duke de Gramont, claiming the right of the Germans, under all recognized international law, to leave France if they wished to do so. It was in vain. But now came a change of ministry. The Prince de la Tour d'Auvergne became Minister of

Foreign Affairs, and the Government took precisely the opposite course, and decided to expel the Germans. Again Mr. Washburne intervened, claiming that this was as much a violation of international law as the other course. All he could obtain was, that the decree should be executed with leniency, and that liberal exceptions should be made in individual cases of special hardship. But the French press called for the expulsion of the Germans, and the Corps Législatif passed a resolution that they should be expelled *en masse*.

As soon as the decree was published in the *Journal Officiel*, and placarded on the walls of Paris, they came in shoals to the Legation. From seven o'clock in the morning till five in the afternoon, when we closed the office, they fairly besieged us. Five hundred often collected in the street at once. We were compelled, though reluctantly, to ask for the aid of the police, both as a protection to the Germans themselves against the mob, and for our own convenience. We had six gendarmes constantly on duty. It was almost impossible to get up our own stairs, and Americans who had business at the Legation complained of the impossibility of getting in. I found a side-entrance through a neighbor's apartment, of which I revealed the secret to some of my countrymen.

The French Government required that every German leaving Paris should be furnished with a pass from us. At Mr. Washburne's request they dispensed with the police *visa*, and so simplified matters. But there were forty thousand Germans in Paris; of these about thirty thousand went away. Allowing three persons to each pass, for many had families, we issued about three thousand passes in six weeks. Many needed assistance to enable them to leave Paris. The Prussian Government, with great liberality, put fifty thousand thalers (thirty-seven thousand five hundred dollars) at our disposition, and this sum they afterward increased. We gave those who needed them railroad tickets to the frontier of Germany and Belgium; there the German Government took charge of them, or rather a charitable organization under the presidency of the Empress Augusta, who showed the most unwearying devotion in good works during the whole war. Eight or ten thousand remained in Paris during the siege. Of those at least one-third came upon the Legation for support, unwillingly in most cases, and driven by necessity.

THE EMPEROR'S STAFF. 149

But while the Germans thus thronged our office, our own countrymen were not wanting. In six weeks we issued eleven hundred passports. Allowing an average of three persons to a passport, thirty-three hundred Americans passed through Paris in those six weeks. To these may be added another thousand who had passports from the State Department. The question has often been asked me, How many Americans do you suppose are in Europe? If to the above forty-three hundred we add seventeen hundred for those who remained quietly where the war found them, or procured their passports at other legations, we have six thousand souls. At that time this was the average number of our people temporarily in Europe. There are fewer now.

On the 28th of July the Emperor started for the seat of war. He took with him his Centgardes and a numerous staff. Nothing can be worse for an army than to be encumbered with a large head-quarters staff. It involves an immense amount of transportation, blocking up the roads, and interfering with the march of the troops. Every thing must give way to head-quarters trains, even supplies for the soldiers and ammunition for the guns. This naturally breeds discontent, and interferes with the efficiency of the army. A staff should consist of the fewest possible number of working men, and they should be restricted, like the line, to a limited amount of baggage. Sherman gave an example of what a staff should be in this respect, on his famous march to the sea.

Meantime rumors of disaster came thick and fast from the front. The French had fought the battle of Wissembourg with great gallantry, but they were outnumbered and outgeneraled. Indeed, it was their misfortune in this war to have no great generals. I was reminded of our own experience when our war broke out, and when we appointed to high command men who had "the Spirit of the Lord, and a disposition to storm works," which Mr. Stanton then declared to be all that was necessary. He lived to change his mind, and to become one of the strongest advocates of trained military talent. Happily for us, the war lasted long enough to enable us to sift the wheat from the chaff. Its close found in high command the very men best fitted to be there. The good sense of our rulers and the tenacity of our people had enabled us to effect this vital change. The French were not so fortunate. Their generals in high command when the war broke out were not equal to the situation, and their armies were defeated and overwhelmed before the officers of ability, who were undoubtedly to be found among them, but in inferior positions, had had the opportunity to show what was in them. For the system of advancement under the Empire was not calculated to bring the best men to the front. I was told during the siege by General Berthaut, now Minister of War, that an officer who studied was looked upon as a republican, and passed over. The road to promotion lay through the *café*.

There were bitter rivalries, too, between the corps commanders. It was stated, I do not know with what truth, that repeated messages failed to bring up the supporting corps to MacMahon's assistance. The same thing had happened at Solferino, where, as it was alleged, the battle was nearly lost, because Canrobert would not support Niel. A challenge passed between them, and nothing but the imperative intervention of the Emperor prevented the scandal of a duel.

The defeat at Wissembourg was not published in Paris till several hours after it had appeared in the London morning papers. The press was muzzled. The depression produced was very great. Certain

Bourse operators took advantage of the inflammable state of public opinion. One day a man in the uniform of a Government courier rode up to the Bourse, and, calling out his confederate, delivered a dispatch purporting to come from the front: "Great victory; total defeat of the Prussians; capture of the Crown Prince; French army in full march for Berlin!" Up went stocks. The crowd shouted, sung, wept for joy, threw themselves into each other's arms, embraced, and kissed. Popular actors and singers were recognized as they drove through the streets, stopped, and compelled to sing or recite the "Marseillaise." Paris was drunk with joy. Then came the reaction. The truth was soon known. As they had been extreme in their joy, they were now extreme in their grief. They were not only despondent, they were in despair. As the poor Empress said at the time to Mr. Washburne, "They have no fortitude." The crowd collected in the streets, inveighed against the Government, and, in a pouring rain, marched to Ollivier's residence, in the Place Vendôme, and insisted upon his addressing them. Ollivier was then the head of the Government. He had not much to say, but he was an eloquent speaker, and partially pacified them.

But the defeats of the French and their consequent exasperation reacted upon the Germans under our protection. Employers discharged their workmen; those who would gladly have kept them dared not. They lived in constant dread, and the number of those thronging to the Legation to obtain the means of departure increased daily. The suffering, both moral and physical, was very great. It must be borne in mind that many of these people had been settled for years in Paris; that they had married there; their children had been born and had married there; their property and their business interests all lay there. Yet they were pitilessly expelled, and not only their business interests ruined, but the dearest family ties dissevered. We have heard much in history and romance of the expulsion of the Moors from Spain, and of the Huguenots from France, and our sympathies are deeply stirred as we read of the misery endured by those poor exiles. I do not see why the expulsion of the Germans does not rank with these touching episodes, both in the suffering of the victims and the pathos of their departure.

Of course the French Government did not expel these poor people with the *cœur léger*. They had their reasons. They said that in case of siege there would be additional mouths to feed, and that it would be a constant source of danger to have so many Germans residing in their midst. But at that time a siege was not anticipated; and, except in this case, there surely could have been no danger in their stay.

There were touching scenes at the Legation among the weeping crowd of women. Some left children and grandchildren married to Frenchmen. Some were not in a fit condition to travel, but required the comforts of a home, and tender care. A child was born upon a bench in the street in front of the Legation. (It was suggested to name it after a distinguished American diplomate.) Every thing that energy and kindness of heart could do to facilitate the departure of those poor people, and to mitigate its severity, was done by our minister.

And here let me remark that no one could have been better fitted for the difficult task he was suddenly called upon to undertake than Mr. Washburne. He trusted to the dictates of a sound judgment, a kind heart, and a fearless temperament; and these are pretty safe guides in the long run. Had he been brought up in diplomacy, he would have hesitated and read up for precedents which did not exist, and so let the propitious moment pass. The result of my observation in Europe during ten years of pretty active service is this: that while there should be a permanent officer in every embassy—a *chancellier*, as he is called in Paris—who can turn promptly to any page of the archives, and is posted in the history of the relations of the country in which he resides with his own; who knows the court ceremonial, and is intimate with the court officials; in short, "who knows the ropes"—it is quite as well that the head of the embassy should be a *new* man. He will attach much less importance to trifles, and act more fearlessly in emergencies. Great Britain and France have pursued this plan in several instances lately. The old diplomates grumble, but it is clearly for the advantage of the country.

News of reverses now poured in upon us, until they culminated in the great disaster of Sedan. That this should have been so great a calamity— a capitulation instead of a defeat—appears to have been the fault of MacMahon. He was compelled by imperative orders from Paris, and entirely against his own judgment, to go to the relief of Bazaine, and to fight against overwhelming odds. But for the tactical disposition of his forces, by which they were penned up in a *cul-de-sac* from which they had no line of retreat, he, as commander-in-chief, is apparently responsible. But the French armies seem from the beginning to have been badly organized, badly led, and conscious that they were so, and discouraged accordingly. I have General Sheridan's authority for saying that the position of the French at Sedan was a very strong one; and while it was inevitable that they should be defeated by superior numbers, they ought to have held their ground for three days. I have no doubt that our troops under Sheridan would have done so. He spoke in the highest terms of the gallantry of the French cavalry, which was sacrificed to encourage the infantry. The remark of a distinguished French general upon the Charge of the Six Hundred, "*C'est magnifique, mais ce n'est pas la guerre,*" would have applied equally well to the charge of the cuirassiers at Sedan.

Sheridan accompanied the King's head-quarters. We had asked officially, at the commencement of the war, that he might be permitted to accompany the French army, and been refused. The Emperor subsequently told Dr. Evans that he had never heard of the application. General orders had been issued that no foreign officer should go with the army; but there was surely some difference between the application of an officer for this permission on his own account, and the request of a friendly Government that the Lieutenant-General of its armies might be permitted to accompany the Emperor. The application probably never got beyond the *chef du cabinet* of the Minister of Foreign Affairs. Nowhere in the world is bureaucracy carried to the extent it is in France. A minister can scarcely appoint a clerk in his office. The *chef du bureau* is omnipotent in his own department. The Republic promised to change all this; but its ministers, after a gallant effort, have fallen in the struggle, and things move on in the same old groove.

At the battle of Sedan, Sheridan stood near Count Bismarck. Toward its close he shut up his glass, and, turning to Bismarck, said, "The battle is won." The Count replied that he should be glad to think so, but saw no signs of it yet. In a minute or two more the French gave way. Turning his glass toward Sedan, Sheridan observed, "The Emperor is there." Bismarck answered that it could not be; that the Emperor was not such a fool as to place himself in that situation. Looking again, Sheridan said, "He is there, anyhow." He had drawn his conclusions from the immense staff he saw, and the confusion reigning among them.

Sheridan was right. The Emperor and his staff were prisoners of war. The Emperor had behaved with the greatest personal courage, and subsequently, when dissensions arose between the French generals as to who was responsible for the great disaster, he behaved with the greatest generosity. But he should not have been at Sedan. The post of usefulness and of danger for him was at Paris, and not with the army.

CHAPTER XIII.

Revolution of September 4th, 1870.—Paris *en Fête*.—Flight of the Empress.—Saved by Foreigners.—Escapes in an English Yacht.—Government of National Defense.—Trochu at its Head.—Jules Simon.—United States recognizes Republic.—Washburne's Address.—Favre's Answer.—Efforts for Peace.—John L. O'Sullivan.

On Sunday, the 4th of September, 1870, Paris was *en fête*. The Parisians had a new revolution, and were delighted with it. The whole population had turned out, men, women, and children, in their holiday clothes. They filled the beautiful Place de la Concorde, the finest in the world; they swarmed across the bridge and into the Palais Bourbon, where the Corps Législatif was in session. The soldiers who guarded the imperial legislators melted away, the cocked hats of the truculent gendarmes vanished miraculously. The Conscript Fathers did not exactly imitate the Roman Senators when they too were invaded by the Gauls, but disappeared as quickly as the gendarmes. These were the gentlemen who had howled for war, and called Mr. Thiers traitor when he pleaded for peace. The people were gay, good-humored, happy; in short, it was a Sunday fête, and in half an hour Paris, and consequently France, was a republic.

From the Palais Bourbon the crowd went to the Tuileries, where the Empress was awaiting the progress of events. There was no anger then felt toward her, and she was not in danger; but a mob, and especially a French mob, is a capricious creature. It may be in the gayest of humors; a trifle turns its mood, and it becomes blood-thirsty as a tiger. The Empress sent for Trochu, the Governor of Paris. He had sworn on his faith as a soldier, a Catholic, and a Breton, to stand by her to the end. He kept his word by sending an aid-de-camp to her assistance. Of all the creatures of the court whom the favor of the Emperor had raised from obscurity, not one came near her. Jerome Bonaparte—the American Bonaparte—had been Governor of the Palace. Fortunately he had been appointed to the command of a regiment of cavalry; for had he still been Governor there would probably have been a fight, and it was as well that there should be no bloodshed. Happily for the Empress, two foreigners remembered her. The Embassador of Austria and the Minister of Italy went to her aid. They found every sign of demoralization at the palace, the servants deserting, and pilfering as they went. They persuaded her, much against her will, to fly. They traversed the whole length of the Louvre to the door in the rear. Metternich opened the door, but, seeing the crowd, closed it again. "*Ce n'est que l'audace qui sauve,*" said the Empress, and ordered it opened. They passed into the crowd. A *gamin* recognized her, and cried, "*L'Impératrice! l'Impératrice!*" "I'll teach you to cry '*Vive la Prusse!*'" said Nigra, and pinched his ear till he howled. Metternich went for his carriage. While he was gone, a *fiacre* passed, Nigra hailed it, and the Empress and Madame Le Breton entered. It was agreed that they should meet at the house of a noted Bonapartist. She went there, and was refused admission. She went to another; he was out of town. In this emergency she thought of Dr. Evans, her American dentist, and drove to his residence. He was expecting two American ladies on a visit to his family, and every thing was prepared for them. When the servant announced two ladies, the doctor was at dinner. Excusing himself to his guests, he went out to receive them, and found the Empress. The next day he took her and Madame Le Breton in his carriage to Trouville, on the coast, near Havre. There was a sort of guard kept at the gates of Paris, though not a very strict one. The doctor said, "You know me, Dr. Evans. I am taking this poor lady to the asylum here at Neuilly." They passed, and arrived safely at Trouville, where the doctor's family were spending the summer.

In the mean time a little English yacht of fifty tons was lying in dock at Trouville. Her owner, Sir John Burgoyne, great-nephew of General Burgoyne, who commanded the British troops at Saratoga, had intended to sail that day for England; but at the suggestion of an American lady, a friend of his wife's, had decided to remain another day, and make an excursion to the ruins of the castle of William the Conqueror. In the evening Dr. Evans went on board, and stated who he was, and what he had come for. As soon as he was satisfied that the Empress was really at Trouville, Sir John said that he would gladly take her across the Channel, and it was agreed that she should come on board in the morning, when the tide served. That evening the gendarmes visited the yacht, for it was rumored that the Empress was at Trouville. In the morning she came on board, and the yacht sailed. The voyage was very rough, and the little vessel was obliged to lie to. She arrived safely at Ryde, however, and the Empress proceeded at once to Hastings, where she met her son. Thus she had escaped by the aid exclusively of foreigners—an Austrian and an Italian, an American and an Englishman.

The new Government, the "National Defense" they called it—the French attach great importance to names—was duly inaugurated at the Hôtel de Ville. Had it not been inaugurated there, and proclaimed from the historic window, the Parisians would scarcely have looked upon it as a legitimate Government. General Trochu was placed at its head, and Jules Favre made Minister of Foreign Affairs. The appointment of Trochu was unfortunate. He was an honorable man, intelligent, a student, and a good military critic, but utterly valueless in active service. He coddled the mob, treating them as if they were the purest of patriots; whereas they were the marplots of the Defense. He was selected probably because he was the only Republican among the French generals of prominence, and not for any peculiar fitness for command in those troublous times.

Shortly after the inauguration of the Government

of the National Defense, Mr. Washburne had occasion to go to the Hôtel de Ville. Jules Simon, now Minister of the Interior, seized the opportunity to make us an oration. What particular object he had in view, unless it were to convince the Minister of the United States that Jules Simon was a great orator, I have been unable to discover. If that was his object, he succeeded. Whether it was worth while to occupy his and our valuable time for this purpose only, may be doubted.

On the 7th of September came our instructions to recognize the Republic if it seemed to us to be firmly established. Mr. Washburne sent me to make an appointment with Jules Favre. It was made for that afternoon. While Washburne prepared his address, I read up in the archives of the Legation to learn what was done under similar circumstances in 1848. I found that we had been the first to recognize the Republic at that date, but that Lamartine, in his report, had taken no notice of the fact, for fear, it was said, of wounding the susceptibilities of Great Britain. Washburne told me to mention this circumstance to Favre: he did not intend that we should be ignored a second time, if he could prevent it. I mentioned it to Favre, and he replied, substantially, that Great Britain had not treated France so well that they need have any particular anxiety about wounding her susceptibilities; and added that Great Britain was now of very little consequence.

Mr. Washburne's address was an admirable document. Favre replied to it very happily. He said that the recognition of the "young Republic" by the United States was a *"grand appui;"* that he "felt gratitude and profound emotion." Jules Favre is a master of the French language. It is a great treat to hear him, even in ordinary conversation, roll out in a charming voice and impressive manner the most perfectly harmonious words of that beautiful language. French does not rise to the sublimity of poetry. Shakspeare is absurd in French. But for charm in conversation, and precision in science, it is simply perfect.

The next day the interview was reported in full in the *Officiel.* Washburne's address was very well translated, except where he quoted from the Declaration of Independence, and spoke of the right of every man to "life, liberty, and the pursuit of happiness." Here the translator had made him say that every man had a right *"de vivre en travaillant au bonheur de tous.*" Rather a liberal translation, and thoroughly French both in language and sentiment. But I have not remarked that the French Republicans labor more for the happiness of their neighbors than other nationalities, or than their own countrymen. If there be a political party in France which does more in charities than another, it is the Orleanist.

Favre was very anxious that Mr. Washburne should intervene to make peace. When he found that under our instructions we could not join with other European powers in political matters purely European (advice left us by Washington, and wisely followed by Mr. Fish), he begged Mr. Washburne to intervene in his private capacity. But he replied very sensibly that it was impossible for him to separate his private from his public capacity; he must always be the Minister of the United States.

But what Washburne felt compelled to decline, another American gentleman, Mr. O'Sullivan, formerly our Minister at Lisbon, undertook. He asked Mr. Washburne for a letter to Bismarck, but this he did not feel authorized to give. He then begged for a letter of introduction to Sheridan, who was at the King's head-quarters. This he received. Jules Favre, who clutched eagerly at any thing that might possibly lead to peace, gave him a safe-conduct, and he started for the Prussian lines. But he never got to head-quarters. That long-headed Bismarck had anticipated some such outside benevolent efforts, and had given orders to the outlying corps that if any distinguished gentlemen came along desiring to make peace, they should be treated with all possible courtesy, but not allowed to approach head-quarters without permission of the King. O'Sullivan was stopped, and his letter forwarded to Sheridan. Bismarck sent for the General, and asked if he knew O'Sullivan. He said he did not. He then asked if he was anxious to see him. Sheridan replied that he should be happy to make his acquaintance, but that he saw no pressing haste in the matter. "Then he sha'n't come," said Bismarck; and O'Sullivan returned to Paris. But the French did not treat him so well as the Germans. As he approached Paris, walking quietly along the high-road, a carpet-bag in one hand and an umbrella in the other, a detachment of the vigilant National Guard rushed across a field and covered him with their loaded pieces. As he made no resistance, they simply took from him his bag and umbrella, and led him before their commander blindfolded. That officer sent him under guard to one of those wretched dens scooped out of the barrier where they sometimes confined smugglers temporarily, but which were oftener used for more unsavory purposes. There they kept him all night. In the morning Jules Favre sent to his assistance, and he was released.

O'Sullivan afterward left Paris in the general exodus of Americans. He went, as they did, to Versailles; but he staid there some three weeks, talking peace to the German princes quartered at the Hôtel des Réservoirs, some of whom he had previously known. He had a plan, not at all a bad one in itself, but under the circumstances entirely impracticable. It was to neutralize a strip of territory lying between France and Germany, annex part of it to Belgium, and part to Switzerland, and put it under the protection of the Great Powers. One evening O'Sullivan dined with the Crown Prince. He sat next to Bismarck, and discoursed upon his pet neutral-strip theory. As they parted, Bismarck shook his hand, and said that he was charmed to make his acquaintance. "But, Mr. O'Sullivan, a curious thing sometimes happens to me: I make the acquaintance of a most agreeable gentleman in the afternoon, and in the evening I find myself reluctantly compelled to order him out of Versailles." O'Sullivan mentioned this to friends he was visiting in the evening, but did not see its application to himself. They did, however. He went to his hotel, and found a Prussian officer at his door with orders for him to leave Versailles that night. He remonstrated, and it was finally agreed that he should start at eight o'clock in the morning. A sentry was placed at the bedroom door, who thought that a proper discharge of his duty required him to open it every five minutes during the night, to make sure that his prisoner had not escaped. Mrs. O'Sullivan did not quite appreciate the situation.

CHAPTER XIV.

Belleville Demonstrates.—Radical Clubs.—Their Blasphemy and Violence.—Unreasonable Suspicion.—Outrages.—Diplomatic Corps.—Some of them leave Paris.—Meeting of the Corps.—Votes not to Leave.—Embassadors and Ministers.—Right of Correspondence in a Besieged Place.—Commencement of Siege, September 19th.—Besiegers and Besieged.—Advantages of Besieged.

BELLEVILLE now began a series of patriotic demonstrations at the Legation, which soon became a nuisance. When I first heard the drum and fife coming up the Rue Chaillot, and several respectable-looking citizens came in and inquired for Mr. Washburne, I was quite impressed with the interest of the occasion. Washburne went out upon the balcony and made them a speech, and thanked them for this *démonstration patriotique.* But when they began to come daily, and the rag, tag, and bobtail at that, and day after day Washburne was called out to thank them for this *démonstration patriotique*, I got very heartily sick of it. We were too busy to have our time wasted in this way. But as the siege progressed, and we did our duty in protecting the

Germans, as we received news from the outside when others did not, and that news was uniformly unfavorable to the French, the *démonstrations patriotiques* ceased; and it was only a fear of the law, and that "divinity that doth hedge in a" diplomate, that prevented our receiving a demonstration of a very different sort.

For the clubs were now rampant, another bane of the Defense. Had they been suppressed at the beginning, as they were at the end, of the siege by General Vinoy, the result might have been different. Their orators advocated the wildest and most destructive theories amidst the applause of a congenial audience. Blasphemy was received with special favor. I remember once, however, the orator seasoned his discourse too high even for that audience. He said he "would like to scale heaven, and collar [*empoigner*] the Deity." It was the day of balloons, and a wag in the audience called out, "Why don't you go up in a balloon?" This turned the laugh upon the orator, and he disappeared, for in Paris ridicule kills.

A curious and annoying feature in the Parisian character during the war was the unreasoning and unreasonable suspicion of the population. A gentleman from Philadelphia interested in Fairmount Park, which was then just opened, was struck with the beauty of the gates at the entrance to the *Bois* on the Avenue de l'Impératrice — Avenue du Bois de Boulogne they call it now, certainly not a change for the better, for it was a beautiful avenue, appropriately named after a beautiful woman. Our Philadelphia friend called his daughter's attention to the gates, remarking that they would be appropriate at Fairmount, and took out his note-book to sketch them. He was at once surrounded by a mob, he and his daughter arrested, and hurried before the *Maire* of the arrondissement. They said he was a Prussian spy, and was sketching the fortifications. He explained who he was, and what he was doing, and offered the drawing in proof. There were the gates to speak for themselves, but this was no evidence to them. Mr. Justice Shallow insisted that he must be a spy. Happily for him, the mayor's clerk was a sensible man, and spoke a little English, and through his instrumentality our friend was discharged.

I have seen a mob collect about a gentleman who took from his pocket a piece of paper and a pencil to write down an address. I knew an American friend to be arrested, mistaken for Mr. Schneider, formerly President of the Corps Législatif. My man was dark, and Schneider was fair; but that made no difference. During the petroleum madness, immediately after the suppression of the Commune, an American lady was followed to her home and very nearly maltreated because she had a bottle of *fleur d'orange* in her hand, which she had just bought at the druggist's. Our vice-consul had red curtains in his sitting-room. One evening he was disagreeably surprised by a visit of armed National Guards. They accused him of making signals to the enemy. On seeing the red curtains, they became satisfied. That a five-story house on the opposite side of a narrow street must effectually preclude his lights from being seen at a distance, was no answer to them. Mr. Washburne called the attention of the French Government to this outrage; but, as no harm had been done, we could not follow the matter up. Under our consular convention with France, a consul's house is inviolable; but a vice-consul has no official existence when the consul is present. When he is absent, his deputy succeeds to his privileges and immunities as consular representative of the country.

Mr. Washburne was not the man to submit to any

outrage upon German or American property. A squad of National Guards entered and partially pillaged the house of the German school-master Hedler, where Washburne's son and other American boys were at school. Our Minister was in arms at once. The Government apologized, the battalion was paraded under arms, the Chief of Police made them a speech, the guilty men were called out and punished, and full damages were paid to Hedler, assessed to Mr. Washburne's satisfaction.

To resume my narrative. On the 18th of September, several of the principal members of the diplomatic corps left Paris. Their departure gave rise to a good deal of discussion, and much has been written and said upon the subject. The diplomatic corps, as a body, never left Paris. A few days before the siege, Lord Lyons called upon Jules Favre. Favre suggested that if the diplomatic corps wished to leave Paris—and it was natural that they should—he was prepared to accompany them. Lord Lyons replied that he saw no necessity for departure at that time. Favre thereupon said that, in this case, he should stay too.

On the morning of the 18th, Prince Metternich, the Austrian Embassador, came very early to the

British Embassy, and said that he meant to go away that afternoon in company with the Turkish Embassador and the Italian Minister, and hoped that Lord Lyons would accompany them. Lord Lyons replied that he saw no necessity for haste, for Bismarck would let them go at any time. Metternich answered, "I don't want to ask any favors of Bismarck, and my Government doesn't want me to." Lord Lyons then finding that the Great Powers of Europe had left, or were about to leave, Paris, consented to go too, and called again upon Favre. But Favre told him that he had then made his arrangements to stay; but that he should send Count Chaudordy to represent his department at Tours.

As soon as it was known that the representatives of several of the Great Powers had left Paris, a meeting of the corps was called by the Nuncio, at the request of several of its members. The question was put, Shall the diplomatic corps leave Paris? and decided in the negative.

But the members departed one by one, till but a few were left. Another meeting was then called, and again it was decided not to leave Paris.

It is quite generally supposed that Mr. Washburne was the only Minister who remained during the whole siege. This is incorrect. There were six in all—the representatives of Northern powers—Norway and Sweden, Denmark, Holland, Belgium, Switzerland, and the United States. In their relations to the French Government, and in their correspondence with Count Bismarck upon their right to communicate with their respective governments during the siege, and to due notice in case of proposed bombardment, these gentlemen acted in unison as the diplomatic corps at Paris.

The division of diplomatic representatives into embassadors and ministers appears to me to be a mistake. It is certainly pleasant for the embassadors. They have the right of direct communication with the sovereign, for they are held to represent the person of their own sovereign, which the ministers do not. At Paris, at the court festivities, they occupied arm-chairs by the side of the Emperor and Empress, while the ministers were seated on benches in a *loge*. They had precedence on the reception-days of the Minister of Foreign Affairs. A minister might have waited two hours; an embassador dropped in, and entered before him. Some of them, like Lord Lyons, did not abuse this privilege. He transacted his business as quickly as possible, and gave place to another. The Turkish Embassador, on the other hand, used to gossip by the hour. That he kept a dozen of his colleagues waiting seemed rather to please him. I once heard Lord Lyons remonstrate with him for doing so, and he giggled as if he thought it rather a good joke. In Prussia this is not permitted: first come, first served, is the rule at Berlin, and it seems to me to be the just one. Mr. Bancroft got this rule established, and deserves great credit for the stout fight he made on the occasion. Count Bismarck is stated to have said that if there had been no embassadors, there would have been no war; for the French Government could not have invented the story that their Embassador had been insulted by the King. However this may be, there can be no doubt that the system leads to the formation of cliques, and, consequently, to separate action by a clique instead of by the whole corps. This is bad under any circumstances, but particularly unfortunate in great emergencies.

In regard to the right of free communication with their respective governments claimed by the diplomatic corps at Paris, Count Bismarck refused to accord it. He argued that if these gentlemen saw fit to shut themselves up in a besieged place when they could go away for the asking, and when the French Government had made provision for this case by establishing a branch of the Government at Tours, they must take the consequences; but as a favor he would permit correspondence if it were left unsealed. Of course the corps declined these terms. To Mr. Washburne he wrote (and Bismarck writes and speaks admirable English) that his position as protector of the North Germans in France entitled him to a different answer; that as an evidence of his gratitude for the fidelity and energy with which the duties of this position had been discharged, it had given him great pleasure to obtain from the King permission for Mr. Washburne to receive a sealed bag containing his dispatches and his private correspondence as often as military necessities would permit.

There has been much difference of opinion expressed as to the right of a diplomatic body voluntarily remaining in a besieged place to receive and answer dispatches in sealed correspondence. Mr. Washburne contended that they had such a right; and in this he was energetically supported by Mr. Fish. I confess, however, that to my mind the right is by no means clear. To me Bismarck's argument is unanswerable. "You see fit to stay when the Great Powers of Europe have gone, and when the French Government has made arrangements for the due discharge of your duties elsewhere. By so doing you put yourselves in the position of other inhabitants of the besieged place, and can claim no privileges not accorded to them." In the case of Mr. Washburne, charged with the protection of the Germans at the request of the German Government itself, the necessity for remaining at Paris may have existed. At all events, if he thought that it did, it did not lie in the mouth of that Government to say that it did not. By choosing as their agent the representative of a friendly and independent power, they left his judgment unfettered as to the manner of discharging his duties. The same remark applies to M. Kern, the Minister of Switzerland, who was charged with the protection of the Bavarians and the Badois. But as regards the other gentlemen, I can not but agree with Count Bismarck. I was confirmed in this view, after the siege was over, by General Sheridan. Dining at my table one day in company with Mr. Washburne, he said to him, "If I had been in Moltke's place, you would not have had your bag."

The siege commenced on the 19th of September. For some days previous the streets of Paris had presented an unwonted and curious appearance. They were thronged with the quaintest-looking old carts, farm-wagons, Noah's arks of every kind, loaded with the furniture of the poor inhabitants of the neighborhood flying to Paris for safety. On the other hand, the stations were thronged with the carriages of the better classes leaving the city. The railroads were so overworked that they finally refused to take any baggage that could not be carried by the passenger himself. Imagine the painful situation of some of our fair countrywomen, Worth's admirers and patrons! To have come to Paris amidst all the dangers of war to procure something to wear, to have procured it, and then to be unable to carry it away! But what will not woman's wit and energy do under such circumstances? A clever and energetic friend of mine hired a *bateau-mouche*, one of the little steamers that ply on the Seine from one part of Paris to another, and, embarking with her "impedimenta," sailed triumphantly for Havre.

It had been agreed between Mr. Washburne and myself that if the diplomatic corps left Paris, and he accompanied them, I should remain to take charge of the Legation, and look after American and German property; and he so reported to Mr. Fish. I had quite a curiosity to be a besieged. I had been a besieger at Port Hudson, and thought that I would like to experience the other sensation. The sensation is not an unpleasant one, especially in a city like Paris. If you have been overworked and harassed, the relief is very great. There is a calm, a sort of Sunday rest, about it that is quite delightful. In my experience the life of the besieged is altogether the most comfortable of the two. You live quietly in your own house, and with your own servants; and with a little forethought you may be amply provisioned. You sleep in your own room, instead of in a cold, damp, and muddy tent; and if an *éclat d'obus*—as the French delicately call it—strikes your house on one side, you move into the other. There has been a great deal of fine writing about famous sieges, and the suffering and heroism of the inhabitants. I imagine that there was not so much suffering, after all, at Saragossa; and that the "Maid" and her companions in arms had plenty of corn-meal and good mule-meat to eat—not a disagreeable or unwholesome diet for a while!

CHAPTER XV.

Balloons.—Large Number dispatched.—Small Number lost.—Worth.—Carrier-pigeons.—Their Failure.—Their Instincts.—*Times* "Agony Column."—Correspondence.—Letters to Besieged.—Count Solms.—Our Dispatch-bag.—Moltke complains that it is abused.—Washburne's Answer.—Bismarck's Reply.

At the beginning of the siege, one of the absorbing topics of discussion among the Parisians was the means of communication with the outer world. The French had always had a fancy for ballooning, and were probably in advance of the rest of the world in this respect. They now applied their experience to a practical use, and soon a service of mail balloons was organized, starting from Paris twice a week. At first they were dispatched in the afternoon, for the all-sufficient reason that they always had been dispatched in the afternoon; but soon they found that the balloon did not rise quickly enough to escape the bullets of the Prussians encamped upon the hills which surround Paris. So they changed the hour of departure to one in the morning. When daylight appeared they were beyond the Prussian lines. Indeed, the speed of the balloon is sometimes marvelous. Starting at one o'clock in the morning, one of them fell into the sea off the coast of Holland at daylight. The passengers were rescued by a fishing-smack. A second descended in Norway on the very morning it left Paris. The officer of the Post-office who was charged with the organization of this service told me that, of ninety-seven balloons that left Paris during the siege, ninety-four arrived safely; about equal to railway-trains in these latter days. Two fell into the hands of the enemy, and one was never heard of. It was supposed to have drifted out to sea and been lost. A balloon was seen off Eddystone Light-house. A few days afterward a gentleman spending the winter at Torquay received a letter from the rector at Land's End, Cornwall, stating that a number of letters had drifted ashore, supposed to have been lost from a balloon, and among them was one addressed to him; that it had been dried, and on receipt of twopence it would be sent him. It proved to be a balloon letter from me, and is still preserved as a souvenir of the siege and the sea.

Quite at the beginning of the siege a member of my own family received a letter from me, dispatched by the first balloon which left Paris. Its arrival created quite a sensation in the little Welsh watering-place where she was spending a part of the autumn. People stopped her in the street, and asked to see the "balloon letter." The natives evidently thought that it must have something of the balloon about it.

I recollect Worth's coming to the Legation one day—(and who does not know Worth? He rules the women throughout the civilized and toileted world; and through the women he rules the men, or their pockets at least). Worth was in great distress. His nephew had gone out in a balloon and been captured, and there were rumors that his life was in danger. I promised to ascertain his fate, if possible, and prepared a letter to Count Bismarck, which Mr. Washburne signed. Bismarck replied most promptly, as he always did. And here let me state that during the siege, at the request of anxious wives and parents, we often addressed inquiries to German Head-quarters to ascertain the fate of a husband or a son, and that these inquiries always received the promptest and kindest attention. To the inquiry about young Worth, Bismarck replied that he had been captured attempting to cross the Prussian lines in a balloon; that to cross the Prussian lines in the air was like crossing them on the land; and that the person caught attempting it would be similarly punished; that young Worth was in prison, and would be kept there for a few months, to teach others not to attempt the same thing; but that no other harm had happened, or would happen, to him. I sent for Worth, and read him the letter. He was much relieved, and expressed himself very grateful. Some years later a relative of mine took the material for a dress to Worth, and asked him to make it up. Think of the audacity of such a request! But Worth did it. If gratitude is to be measured not by the magnitude of the favor conferred, but by the sacrifice made by him who confers it, then Worth's gratitude stands out in unequaled grandeur.

But while with the help of balloons the Parisians managed very well to send letters from Paris, it was no easy task to receive them. The pigeon experiment proved a failure. No doubt pigeons can be trained to do their work tolerably well, and the French Government now has a large collection of carriers at the Jardin d'Acclimatation. But during the siege very few succeeded in reaching home. A carrier will scarcely ever make a two days' journey.

If night overtakes him, he goes astray, misled perhaps by siren wood-pigeons. In winter, too, the days are short, snow-storms blind him, and hawks pounce upon him. One of the canards circulated in Paris was that the Prussians trained hawks for this purpose. The instinct of the animal, too, seems to teach it to fly northward only. Two or three times a carrier arrived safely, bringing with it one of those marvels of scientific skill, a photographic letter. The microscope revealed the contents of a good-sized newspaper transferred to a scrap of paper that a pigeon could carry under its wing.

Some of the French residing in London took advantage of the "agony column" of the *Times* to send news to their friends. They had faith in the ubiquity of the great journal, and their faith was rewarded. I doubt if you could so hedge in a city that the *Times* would not penetrate it. Our Legation in London sent it to us. I received one number a week. In it I found multitudes of *prières* addressed to Mr. Washburne, and some to myself, begging us to inform Mr. So-and-so, or Madame Blank, that their wife, or husband, or children, were at such and such a place, and all well. When these messages were purely personal, we delivered them. If they were in cipher, or susceptible of a double meaning, we did not. I remember finding a message in cipher, and addressed to the Minister of War. I not only did not deliver it, but I burned it for fear that the favor of receiving our letters and papers accorded us by the German Government might be abused. About two days before the *jour de l'an*, I received a *Times* of December 23d, for the Germans purposely delayed our bag, probably that the news, should it become known to the French Government, might not be acted on by it, to the detriment of German military operations. The "agony column" was full of messages to besieged relatives. I thought that the Parisians could receive no more acceptable presents for their New-year's-day, so I copied all the messages which had addresses and sent them by mail. But some had no addresses. How the writers ever expected them to reach their destinations, I do not understand. I copied them too, however, and sent them to the *Gaulois*. On New-year's morning that journal published them. In a few days it received grateful letters, thanking the editors warmly, and offering to pay a share of the expense, "which must have been great." The *Gaulois* replied, declining all payment, but modestly assuming great credit to itself for its "unparalleled enterprise," and assuring its correspondents that it should continue to spare no expense to procure them news of their families.

The Prussian officers, too, at head-quarters not unfrequently sent in letters, with the request that we would distribute them. I remember once receiving from Count Solms, who had been *chargé d'affaires* at Paris after the departure of the Embassador, a letter forwarded by him, without address, without signature, and without date. I waited a few days, thinking that other letters might refer to it, and that the owner would call and claim it. No one came. As the difficulties increased, of course I was the more determined to trace out the owner. Every thing else failing, I read the letter, to try to obtain a clue. Fortunately, I found the name of Mr. Henri Blount. I knew Mr. Blount, and knew that his father was in Paris. I wrote him, and told him the circumstances. He replied that if I would trust him with the letter, he thought that he could find the owner. He took it to the Jockey Club at dinner-time, and asked if there was any gentleman there whose name was Charles, and whose wife's name was Anna. A gentleman immediately claimed it, but after a glance reluctantly gave it up. Another claimed it, and turned out to be the right man.

I had rather an amusing correspondence with Count Solms in reference to this letter and other matters. I give two or three of the letters which passed between us, as showing that we contrived to enjoy ourselves after a fashion in Paris, notwithstanding the rigors of the siege. I give the letters as written. One of them is, perhaps, better adapted to the French language than to its more austere sister English.

"Paris, le 13 Décembre, 1870.

"Mon Cher Comte,—Votre lettre n'est pas vraiment d'un "intérêt palpitant," mais vous êtes bien disciplinés vous autres Prussiens, et j'adore la discipline. Nous voyons les résultats.

"Néanmoins, il puisse être permis à un neutre de vous remercier de vos anxiétés à son égard. Mais il ne meurt pas absolument de faim. J'ai dîné, il y a quatre jours, chez un restaurateur bien connu, en compagnie de quatre jeunes gens que vous connaissez bien. Nous avons mangé un cochon-de-lait, un canard rôti, des truffes et du beurre frais. Ce n'est pas la famine ça—tout arrosé de Château Margaux de '50. Ne croyez pas que dans ces temps ci j'ai commandé un tel dîner de Sybarite moi-même. J'ai été invité. Voilà pourquoi je ne puis rien vous dire de l'addition.

"J'espère qu'on ne trouvera rien de compromettant dans cette lettre excepté pour le cochon-de-lait. Lui il a été bien compromis.

"Je suis toujours à vos ordres pour envoyer des lettres de famille de vos amis.

"Votre dévoué, etc., etc., etc.

"Comme je plains vous autres pauvres Prussiens enfermés hors de Paris!"

"Versailles, le 17 Décembre, '70.

"Mon Cher Colonel,—Merci de votre amusante lettre. Le menu qu'elle contenait m'a complètement tranquillisé, et la solidité de votre repas me fait espérer que vous jouissez encore des forces physiques nécessaires pour que je puisse me permettre de vous prier de vouloir bien vous charger de la distribution des lettres que j'ai l'honneur de vous envoyer ci-joints. Mille amitiés de votre très-discipliné,

"F. Solms."

"Paris, le 25 Décembre, '70.

"Mon Cher Comte,—J'ai reçu votre billet du 17, et je me suis hâté d'envoyer les lettres y incluses. Quelques-unes j'ai livrées moi-même; les autres je les ai mises à la poste.

"Depuis le repas dont la solidité a tant frappé votre esprit, je suis heureux de vous dire que j'ai mangé quelques-uns encore plus solides. Que pensez-vous de lard salé aux haricots — pas verts? Je me suis trouvé transporté aux premiers jours de notre petite guerre en Kansas, au Grand-Ouest, il y a 16 ans.

"Nous avons une nouvelle idée à Paris, une idée tout-à-fait parisienne. Connaissez-vous la cause de la guerre ? Evidemment non. Eh bien, la Providence a trouvé que les vieilles races d'Europe commencent à se dégénérer. Elle désire les mélanger un peu. Il y a probablement 350,000 soldats français prisonniers en Allemagne ; il y a peut-être 600,000 soldats allemands sur le territoire français. Vous voyez, ou plutôt vous verrez, les résultats. Voilà l'idée que j'ai entendu développée avec beaucoup d'éloquence par la belle marquise de ―― à une petite soirée où j'ai eu l'honneur d'assister il y a quelques jours. Je la livre, gratuitement bien entendu, au George Bancroft de l'avenir—'La cause et les résultats de la guerre de 1870.'

"Vous voyez que nous tâchons de nous amuser encore à Paris.

"Agréez, etc., etc., etc."

To be in exclusive receipt of news during a siege is gratifying to one's vanity, but it has its decidedly disagreeable side. I doubt if the siege were to begin again if Mr. Washburne would accept a bag containing any thing but his official dispatches and his family letters. If we gave the Parisians news, they said that we gave them only bad news. If we withheld it, they said that we were withholding the news of French victories. I speak of what was said in the workmen's clubs, and by the inferior press; the better classes and the more respectable newspapers found no fault. Then General Moltke complained that we abused our privilege. His scouts had intercepted a balloon letter, in which the writer spoke of the facility of receiving letters through the Legation, and instructed her correspondent to write under cover to me. That clever writer, too, Labouchère, "The Besieged Resident," told in the columns of the *Daily News* how small a matter it was to be shut up in Paris. "Go to the Legation of the United States on any day, and there you find the latest London journals lying on the table." All this was nuts to General Moltke, for he had opposed our receiving our bag, but had been overruled by the King on the request of Count Bismarck. Bismarck wrote to Mr. Washburne, calling his attention to Moltke's complaint. Washburne replied. After stating the circumstances under which I had authorized a letter to be sent under cover to me, for an American lady whose daughter was sick with the small-pox at Brussels, he proceeded to say that both he and I had endeavored honorably to discharge our duties as neutrals; that we had acted according to the best of our judgments under this sense of duty; that we proposed to continue to act as we had done; and that if the German authorities could not trust us, they had better stop the bag altogether, with the exception, of course, of the dispatches from our Government. At the same time he sent back nearly five hundred letters which had been sent us without authority, and which had not been delivered, as the best possible proof that he had not abused his privilege. Washburne's letter concluded as follows:

"Before closing this communication, I trust your Excellency will pardon me a further observation. For the period of six months I have been charged with the delicate, laborious, and responsible duty of protecting your countrymen in Paris. Of the manner in which these duties, having relation to both belligerents, have been performed, I do not propose to speak. I am content to abide by the record made up in the State Department at Washington. But I can state that there has never been a time when these duties have involved graver consequences and responsibilities than at the present moment. As I have expressed to you before, I have been astonished at the number of Germans who, as it turns out, were left in the city when the gates were closed. Having exhausted their last resources, and finding themselves in a state of the most absolute destitution, they have applied to me for protection and aid, which I have so far been enabled to extend to them from the funds placed in my hands by the Royal Government. The number of these people amounts to-day to two thousand three hundred and eighty-five; and it is certain, had there not been some one to protect and aid them, many must have inevitably perished of cold and starvation. My position in relation to these people and to your Government is known to the people of Paris, and as the siege wears on, and the exasperation is intensified, I now find myself exposed to the hostility of a certain portion of the population of the city. While your military authorities seem to be agitated by the gravest fears in relation to my dispatch-bag, I am daily violently assailed by a portion of the Paris press as a "Prussian representative" and a "Prussian sympathizer;" and a short time since it was proposed in one of the clubs that I should be hanged—rather a pleasant diversion in these dreary days of siege through which we are passing.

"I will only add that, so long as I am the diplomatic representative of my country in Paris, I shall discharge every duty, even to the end, and in the face of every circumstance, that I owe to my own Government, and every duty that I have by its direction assumed toward the subjects of the North German Confederation.

"I have the honor, etc., etc."

Bismarck replied with an apology. He said he knew that the privilege accorded us had not been abused, and he was satisfied that it would not be; that the military authorities had called his attention to this matter, and that it was therefore his duty to call Mr. Washburne's attention to it; that the bag would continue to be sent as usual; and that he returned the five hundred letters, with full authority to Mr. Washburne to deliver them if he saw fit. I heard afterward that Bismarck was delighted with Washburne's letter, and took special pleasure in sending a copy to General Moltke.

CHAPTER XVI.

Burnside's Peace Mission. — Sent in by Bismarck. — Interview with Trochu. — The Sympathetic Tear. — Question of Revictualment. — Failure of Negotiations. — Point of Vanity. — Flags of Truce. — French accused of Violation of Parole. — Question of the Francs-Tireurs. — Foreigners refused Permission to leave Paris. — Washburne insists. — Permission granted. — Departure of Americans. — Scenes at Creteil.

EARLY in the month of October we were surprised by a visit from General Burnside. He happened to be at Versailles, more from curiosity than any other motive, where, through General Sheridan, he became quite intimate with Count Bismarck. Bismarck asked him one day if he would like to go into Paris on a peace mission. Lord Granville had been very urgent with the King to grant the French an armistice, and had induced him to offer it, with a view to an election. There would be no difficulty, Bismarck said, on any point except that of revictualment. This General Moltke would not hear of. Not an ounce of food should enter Paris. "Now," said Bismarck, "that Government of the National Defense is not the wisest in the world, but they are not such d—d fools as to stand out on a point like that. There will be an armistice, and an armistice means peace. If there is peace, England will get the credit of it; and as the United States represents us, I would rather that you had the credit of it." Burnside came in accordingly, accompanied by Mr. Paul Forbes, who was promoted to the rank of aid-de-camp for the occasion, and dubbed a colonel. The Prussians could not realize the idea of a general traveling without his aid. A meeting was appointed with Trochu, and I went as interpreter. His headquarters were at the Louvre, in a large and convenient apartment, occupied, under the Empire, by M. Rouher. Before Burnside had stated the object of his visit, Trochu made us a speech. He spoke well for nearly half an hour. He told us that France had been very wicked; that she had fallen away from the true Catholic faith; that infidelity and skepticism were rampant in the land; that the misfortunes which had come upon her were deserved; that they were visitations for the sins of the people; but that, when they had repented and humbled themselves, he had faith that the punishment would pass from them. He continued in this strain for full twenty minutes, speaking very eloquently; then pulled out his handkerchief, and saying, " Excuse my emotion," he wept. After this he came to business. Burnside confined himself most conscientiously to the exact tenor of his message. Trochu made repeated suggestions of such and such possibilities, but Burnside refused to follow him. He knew nothing but his instructions. As I had feared, Trochu bristled up at the no-revictualment clause. "Such a condition had never been heard of. From the most remote antiquity, there had always been revictualment allowed in case of armistice, so much per head per diem." He gave us at that time no positive answer, but said he would discuss the matter with his colleagues. Negotiations failed upon this very point. The French Government called it a point of honor. It was rather a point of vanity. We did not need the provisions, as the result showed we had food enough for three months. Yet, for that barren privilege of bringing in food which was not needed, the Government of the National Defense rejected the armistice. They could then have made peace, with the loss of one province and two milliards. They continued the war, and lost two provinces and five milliards (one thousand millions of dollars).

It must be remembered that the members of the Government of the National Defense were self-appointed. They were always preaching of their earnest desire to appeal to the people. Here was the opportunity, and they rejected it. It is a pleasant thing to appoint yourself and your particular friends rulers of a great country like France, and one does not readily resign the position. The people might not re-appoint you.

As we left the Louvre, I said to Burnside, "If France is to be saved, it will not be by that man." "I don't know that—I don't know that," he replied. He was evidently impressed by Trochu's eloquence and emotion, and ready tear.

It has been stated that Bismarck refused to enter into negotiations with the Government of the National Defense; that he would not recognize its self-assumed authority, and considered that there was no evidence that it was recognized by the majority of the French people; for there were riots in the great cities of the South, and disturbances in Brittany. Bismarck recognized it or not, as suited his policy, and that policy was exclusively the interests of Germany. Had Trochu waived the food question, Bismarck would have promptly recognized him and his colleagues, so far, at least, as to make an armistice with them, as he afterward did.

Burnside returned that afternoon to Versailles. I accompanied him as far as Sèvres. Trochu sent a carriage for us. It was odd to find one's self in one of the old imperial barouches, drawn by the famous post-horses of the Emperor. We drove through the Bois by Rothschild's house, and so to the broken bridge at Sèvres. In the Bois desolation reigned. The trees were cut down within three hundred yards of the ramparts, the roads torn up and torpedoes planted in them. The swans had gone to feed the hungry soldiers, and the ducks, to avoid the same fate, kept wisely out in the middle of the lake. When we had reached the bridge, a bugle sounded on the French side, and a white flag was displayed. It was soon answered from the German side, and a similar flag was raised. At once the French troops lounged from under cover, their hands in their pockets, and down to the water's edge. The Prussians were kept concealed. They saw us, no doubt, but not one of them was to be seen. Presently, a Prussian officer descended the street, followed by a flag-bearer. He stalks across the bridge to the broken arch, turns, takes the flag from the bearer, and plants the staff in the bridge, with an air as if to say "Touch that, if you dare." The French soldiers are evidently impressed. They mutter, "*Voici des militaires.*" The officer asks in French, "Are those the American generals?" "They are." "Then let them pass." Burnside requests permission to take Antoine with him, the messenger of the Legation. "Is he an American?" "Yes." "Then he can come, of course." The steam-launch puffs up, and the party cross. I cross with them, but return at once to the French side. The soldiers disappear, the flag is lowered, and the firing recommences. I have been rather minute in this description, as the same ceremonies were observed twice a week, when we sent and received our dispatch-bags.

The German Government complained on several occasions of the violation of flags of truce. These complaints were addressed to the French authorities through us. Indeed, every communication addressed to the French Government and its replies were sent through the Legation. This kept us busy even during the quiet days of the siege. The violation of parole was another fruitful source of correspondence. The Germans sent us a list of over twenty-five officers, whom they alleged had broken their paroles.

In some cases—that of General Ducrot, for instance—there are two sides to the question. He claimed that it was a legitimate escape, and the French press was unanimously of his opinion. There was another branch of correspondence that occupied a good deal of our time. The two governments, to their credit be it spoken, did not allow the war to interfere with the administration of justice. Under their treaties each Government was bound to serve upon its own subjects all legal documents in civil suits emanating from the courts of the other. This was done throughout the war, and they all passed through our hands.

There was, too, correspondence between the two hostile governments upon other subjects. Among them I recollect one in relation to the Francs-Tireurs. The Germans treated these irregulars as guerrillas. The French remonstrated. The Germans answered that they had no uniform; that they wore the blue blouse, which is the national dress of the French peasant; and that they ought to wear something which could be distinguished at rifle range. I do not remember how the matter was settled, but I believe that the Francs-Tireurs gradually disappeared, absorbed in the Mobiles.

Not long after Burnside's mission I paid a second visit to Trochu. Mr. Washburne had applied to the Germans for permission for Americans and other foreigners to leave Paris. The King accorded it at once. Any American could leave on Mr. Washburne's pass, any other foreigner on the same pass, provided that his name had first been submitted to and accepted by the German authorities. Having obtained this concession, Mr. Washburne next applied to the French Government for its permission. To his surprise, it was refused. He could not understand it. That the Germans should wish to keep in the city a number of "useless mouths" to help consume the provision, was natural, but that the French, who, for the same reason, ought to have wished to get rid of them, should refuse to let them go, was inconceivable. But Washburne was not the man to sit down quietly under a refusal in a matter like this. He insisted that they must go, and should go. Favre was evidently on his side, and we had reason to believe that he was backed by some, at least, of his colleagues. Trochu opposed the departure for fear of the effect upon Belleville. If I had not heard him say so, I could not have believed it.

As Washburne insisted, and Favre was in favor

of the permission being given, an interview was arranged with Trochu. The "Governor of Paris," as he loved to call himself, made us another oration. It was very much a rehash of the first. He then stated that he had been unwilling that the "strangers" should leave Paris; it looked like "rats deserting the sinking ship;" he feared the effect upon Belleville. But out of regard for Mr. Washburne, and in deference to the opinion of some of his colleagues, he would now consent. He added that he would send an aid-de-camp to Belleville, to spread the report that it was the diplomatic corps leaving the capital. I looked at him with astonishment. That he should tell a lie was bad enough, but that he should tell it out of fear of that wretched mob was a degree of weakness I was not prepared for.

Permission having been given, no time was lost in the preparations for departure. On the 24th of October, forty-eight Americans and several Russians went out by Créteil. A number of English started, but were turned back. Their names had not been sent to Versailles in season. Permission was subsequently received, and they left Paris a few days later. We drove to the French outposts, and thence sent forward the flag with an officer of Trochu's staff, and Mr. Washburne's private secretary, Mr. Albert Ward, who was charged with the necessary arrangements on our side. While we waited, a German picket of six men advanced toward us, dodging behind the trees, muskets cocked, and fingers on trigger. I confess I was not much impressed with this specimen of German scouting. It looked too much like playing at North American Indian. There were some twenty traveling-carriages, open and closed, filled with ladies, and piled up with baggage. The party had as little of a military look as can well be imagined, and yet the picket advanced as if they feared an ambush.

The necessary arrangements having been made, we proceeded to the German outposts. Here the Prussian officers verified the list, calling the roll name by name, and taking every precaution to identify the individuals. I heard afterward, however, that a Frenchman of some prominence had escaped disguised as a coachman.

I met here a young American, who was living not far from Versailles, and who was known to Count Bismarck. I gave him a couple of morning papers. That evening he dined with Bismarck, and offered to sell him the papers for a quart bottle of Champagne for the big one, and a pint bottle for the little one. Bismarck offered a quart bottle for both; but my American indignantly rejected the terms: so Bismarck accepted his, and paid the bottle and a half. I record this as perhaps the only diplomatic triumph ever scored against Count de Bismarck.

CHAPTER XVII.

Mob seize Hôtel de Ville.—"Thanksgiving" in Paris.—Prices of Food.—Paris Rats.—Menagerie Meat.—Horse-meat.—Eatable only as Mince.—Government Interference.—Sorties.—Are Failures.—Le Bourget taken by French.—Retaken by Prussians.—French Naval Officers.—Belleville National Guard.—Their Poetry.—Blundering.—Sheridan's Opinion of German Army.

LATE in October, M. Thiers came into Paris on a peace mission, but met with no success. He brought the news of the fall of Metz. There was great excitement in Paris. The mob collected, marched to the Hôtel de Ville, and took possession. They arrested several members of the Government, and shut them up—others escaped. They then proceeded to depose the Government, and to set up one of their own. Ducrot begged Trochu to let him fire on the mob; he could disperse them, he said, in five minutes. The Mobiles were eager to fire; for the Mobiles and the National Guard lived like cat and dog together. Trochu would not consent. The insurgents remained in possession of the Hôtel de Ville all that night, and the next day gradually melted away. It was one of those unfortunate mob triumphs which contributed not a little to the success of the Commune.

The siege found about two hundred Americans in Paris. I ought to say "citizens of the United States;" but we have taken to ourselves the broader title, and in Europe it is generally accorded to us. Of these two hundred about fifty went away, and about one hundred and fifty remained. The French live from hand to mouth, buying only what is necessary for the day, and laying no stores in. This comes, I think, from their system of living in apartments, and the want of store-rooms. The Americans, as a rule, laid in a stock of provisions. The grocers of Paris had imported a large quantity of canned food for the use of the *colonie américaine*, which was then, and still is, a power in Paris. The greater part of the *colonie* having gone, there remained a quantity of canned vegetables, fruit, deviled ham and turkey, oysters, lobsters, etc., etc., and, above all, hominy and grits. The French knew nothing of these eatables till late in the siege, when they discovered their merits. In the mean time the Americans had bought up nearly all there was on hand.

As Thanksgiving approached we determined to

celebrate it, notwithstanding our supposed forlorn condition. Some thirty of us met at a restaurant on the Boulevard, where we feasted on the traditional turkey, or, rather, on two of them, at twelve dollars apiece. Under the circumstances, we had quite an Epicurean repast. Mr. Washburne presided, and made a humorous speech, dwelling provokingly on the good things our unbesieged countrymen were then enjoying at home. Professor Shepherd, of Chicago, was present, and made some clever and appropriate remarks. The Professor has written one of the most readable and reliable books upon the siege I have met with.

Prices of food in Paris had now reached their height. Turkeys, as I have said, sold at $12 apiece, chickens at $6, cats $1.60, rats 15 cents, dogs from 80 cents up, according to size and fat. There was a refinement in rats. They were known as the brewery rat and the sewer rat. The brewery rat was naturally the most delicate titbit, and as the siege progressed and but little food found its way into the sewers, the sewer rats diminished wofully in numbers, while their brethren of the brewery increased. I know of no better evidence of the severity of the cold, and the scarcity of food during that winter, than an incident that came under my own observation. I was called by the *concierge* of the building to look at the apartment of an American gentleman, on the floor below me. The rats had made their way with great gymnastic agility into the kitchen; they had thrown down and broken two or three dishes which the cook had imperfectly washed, and on which there remained a little grease. They had then made their way into the salons and bedrooms, had gnawed and burrowed into the sofas and mattresses, and there several lay, dead of cold and hunger.

But there was no time in Paris when money would not buy good food, though it could not buy fuel, for that had been seized by the Government. Very late in the siege a man brought to the Legation a piece of *filet de bœuf* of six pounds, for which he asked four dollars a pound. Mr. Washburne and I did not indulge in such luxuries, living principally upon our national pork and beans, and the poetic fish-ball. A young American happened to be in the office, however, who took it at once, and paid his twenty-four dollars.

In the suburbs of Paris food was more abundant. I breakfasted in December with a French general, who commanded one of the outposts. We had beef, eggs, ham, etc., and, from what I heard, I should say that he and his staff breakfasted as well every day. These noonday breakfasts, by-the-way, ruined the French army. I reached my general's head-quarters at half-past eleven. He and one of his staff were smoking cigars and drinking absinthe. At twelve we breakfasted bountifully, as I have said, and with Champagne and other wines, followed by coffee, brandy, and more cigars. We got through breakfast about three o'clock. This was on an outpost, in presence of the enemy. Had he attacked, what would the general and his staff have been worth? They were very far from being intoxicated, but certainly their heads were not clear, or their judgments sound.

The Prussians soon learned the French habits, and attacked them in the field when they were making their soup. The French soldiers could not catch up their soup and pocket it, and eat it at their leisure. They consequently lost not only their breakfasts, but frequently their cooking utensils too. The Germans, on the other hand, had a liberal ration of meat (*fleisch*—what a disagreeable word!)—one pound and a half per diem. But, meat failing, they always had a German sausage and a piece of bread in their haversacks, and could eat as they marched. Yet such is the power of habit in France, and the strength of tradition, that I suppose the French soldier will continue to all time to prepare his soup, even at the expense of defeat.

Without stirring from Paris, I had the opportunity during the siege to taste as many varieties of wild meat as the greatest of travelers—as Humboldt himself. It was found to be impossible to procure food for the animals at the Jardin d'Acclimatation, and they were sold and killed. They were bought mostly by the enterprising English butcher of the Avenue Friedland. I indulged from time to time in small portions of elephant, yak, camel, reindeer, porcupine, etc., at an average rate of four dollars a pound. Of all these, reindeer is the best; it has a fine flavor of venison. Elephant is tolerably good. Some of my readers may remember the charming twin elephants, Castor and Pollux, who carried children round the Garden on their backs, in 1867 to 1869. They were done to death with chassepots—shot through the head. I eat a slice of Castor. It was tolerably good only; did very well in time of siege. But all these meats are but poor substitutes for beef and mutton; and when travelers tell us of the delights of elephant's trunk or buffalo's hump, depend upon it, it is the hunter's appetite that gives the flavor.

The main-stay of the population, in the way of fresh meat, was horse. These were requisitioned, and every horseholder having more than one was compelled to contribute toward feeding the population. The horses were liberally paid for, so much per pound. Some individuals made a very good thing out of it. They got in with the horse officials. A fine animal, requisitioned from the owner, who knew no better than to send it, appeared at the shambles. One of these gentry, with the connivance of the official in charge, would take him, and substitute an old screw of equal or greater weight. I know an American in Paris who is daily aggravated by seeing at the Bois a beautiful mare he once owned, and whose loss he had deeply deplored, but had been comforted by the reflection that she had perished to feed the starving Parisians.

The horse-meat was rationed and sold by the Government at reasonable prices: nine ounces and a half were allowed per diem to each adult. There is a refinement in horse-meat, as in rats. A young light-gray is tender and juicy. Black is the worst color; the meat is coarse and tough. But horse-flesh is poor stuff at best. It has a sweet, sickening flavor. Some people spoke highly of it as soup; others when *mariné*. The only way I found it eatable was as mince mixed with potato.

From horse-meat to beef is but a slight transition, but one more easily made on paper than on the table in those days. The interference of the French Government in almost every detail of private life is something of which happily we know nothing in this country. You can not cut down a tree on your own land without its permission. During the siege you could not kill your own ox without leave from the Minister of Commerce. If you had providently laid in a larger supply of fuel than he thought you needed, he took possession of it, and paid you Government prices for what was then almost priceless. An American lady resident in Paris had a cow. The cow ran dry, and she wanted to convert it into beef. She came to the Legation to secure Mr. Washburne's intervention to obtain for her permission to kill her own cow. At first it was refused, and it required no inconsiderable amount of diplomatic correspondence and the waste of many pages of good foolscap, with a large expenditure of red tape and sealing-wax, before the permission was obtained.

I have said very little of the sorties from Paris. The subject is not a pleasant one. There were five hundred thousand armed men in Paris, and only three hundred and fifty thousand outside. Yet but one serious sortie was ever made. This was to the south-east, under Ducrot; and the fighting was obstinate, and lasted two days. Ducrot had published a proclamation to the effect that he should come back victorious, or be brought back dead. He was defeated, but marched quietly back nevertheless. We are unaccustomed among Anglo-Saxons to this style of proclamation, and call it bombast. I am told, however, by those better acquainted with the French character than I am, that it has its effect upon the French soldier, and is therefore allowable.

The garrison of Paris should have made a sortie every night, sometimes a thousand men, and sometimes a hundred thousand, and in two or three quarters at once. Their central position gave them every opportunity to do this to advantage. Had they done so, they would soon have worn out the Germans with constant *alertes*, and with comparatively little fatigue to themselves. But this, too, was mismanaged. They surprised and took Le Bourget, a little village to the north-east. Of course we all supposed that it would be strongly garrisoned, and the garrison well supported. Not at all. Two days later the Prussians retook it. The garrison made a most gallant defense, but they were entirely unsupported. Not a regiment of the immense army in Paris came to their assistance. No possible excuse can be given for this abandonment.

The loss of Le Bourget produced great discontent among the Parisians; and Trochu was blamed, and most justly. He made an effort to retake it, but in vain. The sailors, under their gallant officers, made a spirited assault, but were repulsed with great loss; for they were not supported by the soldiers. The officers made every effort to lead them on, but they would not assault.

The French naval officers are a very superior class of men. They compare most favorably with those of any other nation. They are painstaking, intelligent, and well-informed. Under their command the sailors fought gallantly during the war, for there was a large number of them detailed to the army, as they had little to do at sea. They felt strongly the deterioration of their sister service, the army. At Versailles I was once dining at a restaurant near a naval officer. An army officer, accompanied by two non-commissioned officers, entered, called loudly for dinner, and made a great disturbance. They were evidently the worse for liquor. I overheard the naval officer muttering to himself, "*Cette pauvre armée française! cette pauvre armée française!*"

There was always blundering. They had shut up a brigade of cavalry in Paris. Jerome Bonaparte, who commanded one of the regiments, told me he had no idea why he was ordered in, unless it was to eat up his horses. This they proceeded to do so soon as they were fairly trained, and so doubled in value. Trochu organized a sortie to the north-west. Two columns left Paris one night by different gates, and were to take up their positions simultaneously and attack at daylight. He forgot that one road crossed the other, and that one column must necessarily halt for the other to pass. Of course one of them arrived late on the ground, and the attack failed. When a sortie was to be made, a flag was hoisted on Mount Valérien. The Germans soon knew its meaning as well as the French, and prepared accordingly. An intended sortie was known at least twenty-four hours before it took place, and its chances discussed on the boulevards. The National Guard, too, with some honorable exceptions, would not fight. The heroes of Belleville howled to be led against the enemy. They got as far as the barriers, and refused to go farther. "They were enlisted to defend Paris, and they would not go beyond the *enceinte;* the Reactionists wanted to get them out, that they might deliver Paris over to the enemy." There was a popular song they sung as they marched through the streets which perfectly illustrates their sentiments and character:

"Nous partons,
   ons, ons,
Comme des moutons,
Comme des moutons,
Pour la boucherie,
   rie, rie.

"On nous massacra,
   ra, ra,
Comme des rats,
Comme des rats.
Comme Bismarck rira!
   rira!"

An officer commanding a fort applied for re-enforcements to relieve his exhausted men. They sent him a battalion of our Belleville gentlemen. The next day he sent them back, saying they had been drunk and fought in the trenches all night, and that he preferred to get along as well as he could with his overworked garrison.

Trochu planned a sortie to the south-east. It was necessary to cross the Marne. The troops arrived at the appointed hour, but the pontoons did not. A whole day was lost, and the sortie was *une affaire manquée*. Outside, things were nearly as badly managed. No serious effort was ever made to cut the German lines of communication. The railways to the east were all-important to them, not so much for provisions (for they drew these mostly from France), but for ammunition. With the enormous guns in use, the transportation of ammunition was a serious matter, taxing the railroad facilities of the Germans to the uttermost. An interruption might have compelled them to raise the siege. Sheridan, who, being at the King's head-quarters, and treated with the greatest kindness and attention, naturally sympathized with the Germans, could not help exclaiming that if he had been outside with thirty thousand cavalry, he would have made the King * * * Well, it is not worth while to quote Sheridan's exact words; they were a little in the style of the commander of the Imperial Guard at Waterloo; but the substance of them was, that an active officer with a good cavalry force could have so broken up the communications of the German army as to compel it to raise the siege. For the Germans are not particularly handy at repairing a broken road or bridge; and a German general does not, as the rebel soldier said of Sherman, carry a duplicate tunnel in his pocket.

As I am quoting Sheridan, let me here record his opinion of the German army. He *believed* that they were brave soldiers. They were well disciplined, well led, and had every appearance of thorough soldiers; but he could not say so positively, for, so far as his observation went, they had never met with any serious resistance. He looked upon the German army as in no respect superior to one of our great armies at the close of the war—the Army of the Potomac, for instance—except as regards the staff. That was far superior to ours, and to any staff in Europe. Their field telegraph, too, excited his admiration. It had been borrowed from us, but improved.

CHAPTER XVIII.

The National Guard.—Its Composition.—The American Ambulance.
—Its Organization.—Its Success.—Dr. Swinburne, Chief Surgeon.
—The Tent System.—Small Mortality.—Poor Germans in Paris.—
Bombardment by Germans.—Wantonness of Artillery-men.—Bad
News from the Loire.—"Le Plan Trochu."—St. Genevieve to appear.—Vinoy takes Command.—Paris surrenders.—Bourbaki defeated.—Attempts Suicide.

A GENTLEMAN of rank and great historic name, of approved bravery, and who had seen service as an officer in the French army, came one day to the Legation in the uniform of a private. I asked him why he had enlisted, when he could so easily have got a commission. He replied that it was true he could easily have got a company in the National Guard, but before he could know his men, and they could know him, and he could drill and discipline them, they would go into action. Then they would inevitably run away. If he ran with them, he would be held responsible; if he stood, he would be killed. So he had decided to enlist as a private, to stand as long as the rest stood, and to run away when they ran. It struck me that this gentleman was wise in his generation, but that it was not precisely in this way that France was to be saved.

In speaking of the National Guard as I have done, it is proper to state that I speak of the masses, the workmen of Paris, and the *petite bourgeoisie* of most of the arrondissements. There were some few battalions that could be relied upon, some composed in part of the "gentlemen of France;" but they were insufficient to leaven the whole lump. The masses, those who drew a franc and a half per diem for themselves, and seventy-five centimes for their wives, or for the women who lived with them—for the Government of the National Defense had decided that it was the same thing—were the turbulent, unruly, unsoldierly mob I have described.

One of the most interesting and satisfactory features of the siege was the American ambulance. Here were order, system, and discipline. It was located on vacant lots in the Avenue de l'Impératrice. It did better work than any other ambulance in Paris; and there were many of them. A number of the wealthy people of the city gave up their hotels, or parts of them, for this purpose. The Press organized an admirable ambulance, copied as much from the American as circumstances would permit. The Italians started one, and two or three other nationalities. But the American ambulance was the only one organized upon the tent system, which is unquestionably the true one. Fresh air and fresh water are what is needed for the wounded. It is impossible to get fresh air in a building, as you get it in a tent. As Dr. Swinburne expressed it, "The air filters through the canvas."

At the Exposition of 1867 we had a remarkably good exhibition of our ambulance system. It was due to the energy and liberality of Dr. Evans. At the close of the exhibition he bought the whole collection; and when the war broke out, he organized an ambulance association, presented it with this material, and gave it ten thousand francs. Other Americans contributed, and the enterprise was launched. Dr. Swinburne, a distinguished corps surgeon of our army, and afterward Quarantine Officer at Staten Island, happened to be in Paris, traveling for his health and amusement. He gave up his trip, and staid in the city, that he might be of service to the wounded French. He deserves much credit for his humanity. Dr. Johnson, a prominent American physician in Paris, took charge of the medical department. Both of these gentlemen discharged their duties with devotion and skill, and with remarkable success, and without remuneration, except that they were decorated by the French Government. For an American residing at home a decoration is of very little account. In France it is useful. It procures him attention on the railways and at the restaurants. But it has been very much abused of late years. There are about one hundred thousand *décorés* in France, so that they now say it is the correct thing not to be decorated. I never heard of but one individual, however, who refused it, and that was from political motives.

A number of American ladies and gentlemen who remained in Paris offered their services in the ambulance, and were enrolled as volunteer nurses. Among them Mr. Joseph K. Riggs was particularly conspicuous by his skill and devotion. They went upon the field after, or even during, an engagement and picked up the wounded. Indeed, there was quite a contest among the ambulances to get possession of the wounded; for while the number of the sick in Paris was very great, that of the wounded was comparatively small. The medical director of General Ducrot's corps became much interested in our ambulance. He turned over to Dr. Swinburne the charming house of M. Chevalier, the eminent French writer on political economy, and then begged him to take charge of the wounded of his corps. Swinburne used the house as a convalescent hospital when his tents were full.

So successful was his treatment that of the amputated only one in five died; while at the great French ambulance of the Grand Hôtel four in five died. The mortality there was fearful.

The apparatus for warming the tents was simple, but most effective. It had grown up among our soldiers during the war. A hole was made in the ground outside of one end of a long tent, a stove placed in it, and the pipe carried the whole length of the tent in a trench. The result was that the ground was thoroughly dried and warmed, and this warmed the whole tent. I have known the thermometer outside to be at 20° Fahrenheit, while in the tents it stood at 55°. The doctor said that for wounded men well covered up in bed 55° was better than 70°.

The men were well fed, and admirably cared for generally. The French Government put the best of their stores at the disposition of the ambulances, and treated them with the greatest liberality. There was always plenty of canned fruit, jellies, etc., in Paris, so valuable in sickness. The ladies bought these, and brought them to the wounded. Tobacco was provided in the same way for the convalescents.

The American ambulance was soon so well and so favorably known, that I heard of French officers who put cards in their pocket-books, on which they had written the request that if they were wounded they might be carried to *l'ambulance américaine*.

The great drawback we had to contend with was the impossibility of procuring new tents. Dr. Swinburne told me that at home they would have been condemned after a month's use, and new ones substituted. But in Europe the cloth is not to be had. We use cotton cloth, the French use linen. Cotton is lighter, is more porous in dry and fulls in wet weather. The result is that the air filters through it in the one case, and the water does not penetrate it in the other. In the absence of new canvas, the doctor thoroughly fumigated the old from time to time. This answered the purpose tolerably well, but did not exhibit the tent system in its perfection.

We had now reached the middle of January, and

the end of the siege was rapidly approaching. The want of proper food, especially for young children, was producing its necessary results; and the death-rate had risen from about eight hundred—which is the average number of weekly deaths in Paris—to four thousand, and this without counting those in hospital which may be set down at one thousand more. The number of poor Germans supported by the Legation had also increased very greatly, and had risen to twenty-four hundred. We were compelled to hire another room, where the weekly allowance made them was paid and duly entered in books kept for this purpose; for every penny expended was regularly entered and vouched for. The poor German women were obliged to walk two or three miles on those cold winter days; for the workmen's quarter is far from that of the Champs Elysées. Mr. Washburne pitied these poor creatures, and gave them omnibus tickets for the return trip. He bought a cask of *vin ordinaire*, too, and gave a glass of warm sweetened wine to each of them. It did them infinite good.

Provisions were now running short; enough remained for a few days only. Even in this most vital matter there was blundering. A gentleman high placed in the office of the Minister of Commerce, the *ministère* which had charge of the supplies, told Mr. Washburne that there were provisions in Paris to last till March. We could hardly credit it, but it came to us from such high authority that we were staggered. He spoke positively, and said he had seen the figures. After the surrender this gentleman met a mutual friend, and said, "I am afraid your minister must take me for either a liar or a fool. I hope I am neither. The mistake we made at the *ministère* happened in this way: the minister appointed two officers; each was to take an account of all the food in Paris, in order that one account might control the other. When their statements came in, he added them together, but forgot to divide them by two."

Meantime we were being bombarded, but after a very mild fashion. I have since talked with a German general who commanded at the quarter whence most of the shells entered the city. He assured me that there never was the slightest intention to bombard Paris. If there had been, it would have been done in a very different style. The German batteries fired from a height upon a fort in the hollow, and their shells, flying high, entered Paris. Still, when nearly two hundred lives were lost, and shells fell among us for nineteen days, people had a right to say that they were bombarded, and no Parisian will admit to this day that they were not. Artillery-men of all nations become not only very careless, but very wanton. The Germans were eager to hit something, and the public buildings of the Latin Quarter offered a tempting mark to the gunners. I was complaining to a French officer one day of the shameful manner in which the French Government troops during the Commune bombarded the quarter of the Champs Elysées, a quarter inhabited almost exclusively by friends of the Government, who were longing for the troops to come in. He told me that it was due to the wantonness of the artillery-men, and cited an instance which came under his own observation. A gunner at Mount Valérien pointed out to the captain of the gun a cart making its slow way through the distant plain toward Paris, and exclaimed, "O, my officer! see that cart carrying supplies to the enemy." "Where, where?" "There, near that white house." "Give it a shell." He fired, missed half a dozen times, but finally hit. It turned out to be the cart of a poor washer-woman, carrying the week's wash to her customers.

A few days before the surrender bad news came thick and fast. A sortie in the direction of Mount Valérien had been repulsed. Chanzy had been defeated. All hope of aid from that quarter had vanished, and but a few days' provisions remained. Will it be believed that even then Trochu "paltered in a double sense" with the suffering people? He published a proclamation in which he said the "Governor of Paris would never surrender." The next day he resigned, and appointed no successor. When, three days later, the city surrendered there was no Governor of Paris.

But even to the last moment there were people who had confidence in Trochu's proclamation. The Parisians are credulous, and readily believe what they wish to believe. Among the populace there was always a sort of half belief in the "Plan Trochu," which, as he often told us, when all else failed, was to save France. This plan he kept mysteriously to himself, or confided it only to a few bosom-friends. But I had it from a source I thought entitled to belief, that Trochu confidently anticipated a miracle in his favor in return for his devotion. St. Genevieve was to appear and save Paris. It is almost impossible to believe that, in the nineteenth century, and in that skeptical capital, a man of intelligence, cultivation, and varied experience, could be found who believed in a miraculous appearance. of the saint; but Trochu was a strange compound of learning, ability, weakness, and fanaticism, and I have little doubt that he confidently anticipated the personal intervention of St. Genevieve to save her beloved city.

On the 24th of January, Vinoy took command. He suppressed the clubs, seized the violent press, and took other energetic measures. A mob attacked Mazas, and released the prisoners. They then tried the Hôtel de Ville a second time; but they had now a different commander to deal with, and they were beaten off with ease. Mr. Washburne and I happened to be in the neighborhood of the Hôtel de Ville, and saw something of this affair. We did not stay to the end, however, for we felt that it was not the proper place for us, accredited as we were to the Government the mob was attempting to overthrow. Had Vinoy or Ducrot been in command from the beginning, the result might have been different. There was no reason why the National Guard should not have made good soldiers; but they needed a discipline of iron. They were permitted to choose their own officers. This of itself was fatal.

In the beginning of our war in some of the States the company officers were elected by the men. But the men themselves were the first to see the folly of this course, and petitioned that their officers might be appointed by the Executive. Had the officers of the National Guard been appointed by the Government, and when they halted at the barrier and refused to go farther, had a battery been ordered up, and a dozen or so of them shot, "*pour encourager les autres,*" as the French said of Admiral Byng, they might have given a very different account of themselves in their combats with the Germans.

On the 27th of January, with seven days' provisions only in Paris, with every man, woman, and child on the shortest possible allowance, the city surrendered. An armistice was agreed upon, which was not, however, to apply to the armies of the East operating toward Lyons. It is said that the French commander in that quarter was not notified that the armistice did not extend to him. He was attacked, caught napping, and defeated.

If I recollect correctly, it was Bourbaki who was defeated in the East. Bourbaki is the type of the *beau militaire* of the French Empire. A dashing, gallant soldier, he had distinguished himself and gained his promotion by scaling the walls of an Arab town at the head of his troops, armed with a light riding-whip only. But these were not the men then wanted at the head of the French armies. When Bourbaki was defeated, and his army in retreat, making its disorderly way to Switzerland, and needing all its General's care and attention, he attempted to commit suicide. In the German service he would undoubtedly have been tried for desertion. In France every thing is pardoned to a man who acts under the influence of strong emotion; and Bourbaki was never even blamed for leaving his army to its fate.

CHAPTER XIX.

Election in France.—Terms of Peace.—Germans enter Paris.—Their Martial Appearance.—American Apartments occupied.—Washburne remonstrates.—Attitude of Parisians.—The Germans evacuate Paris.—Victualing the City.—Aid from England and the United States.—Its Distribution.—Sisters of Charity.

DURING the armistice an election took place. The Assembly met at Bordeaux late in February, and steps were taken toward peace. All sorts of rumors were current as to the terms, and it was said that they were so severe that France must fight on at all hazards rather than accept them. Ten milliards, it was rumored, were to be paid (two thousand millions of dollars). Alsace and Lorraine and a French colony were to be given up, and a number of French men-of-war made over to Germany. The preliminaries were finally agreed upon: five milliards were to be paid, and Alsace and Lorraine transferred. German troops were to occupy Mount Valérien and to enter Paris, and hold a part of it until peace was definitively signed. The Crown Prince was reported to have been opposed to the troops entering the capital, as humiliating to the French, and not a military necessity; but he was overruled.

On the 1st of March I was awakened by military music. I had not heard any for a long time, the French bands having been broken up. I hurried out, and found that the Germans were entering Paris. First came the traditional Uhlans. The safety with which these troops rode in pairs through a great part of France was a curious feature of the war. They were followed by their supports. Then came a mixed band of about one thousand troops, representing all arms and the different German nationalities. They were sent as an advance-guard to secure and prepare the quarters assigned the troops by the *maires*. In the mean time, the Emperor was holding a review at Longchamps, on the very field where, three years and a half before, he had assisted at the review of sixty thousand French troops by the Emperor Napoleon, and it was not until the afternoon that the main body, the Prussian Guard, the Saxons, and the Bavarians, marched into the city. They occupied the quarter of the Champs Elysées, extending as far as the Place de la Concorde — in all about one-eighth of Paris.

This was a busy day for me. Mr. Washburne was

overrun with *concierges* and servants complaining that the Prussians were occupying American apartments. I went to the mayor of the arrondissement. He said that he had quartered the Germans impartially upon all the householders; that the French law exempted apartments of an annual value of less than one hundred dollars; that in his arrondissement, as I knew, the apartments were either remarkably good or remarkably poor; that the good ones were occupied principally by foreigners, and that the poor ones were exempt. From the mayor I went to the German commander occupying the house of Queen Christine on the Champs Elysées, and was told at his head-quarters that they had nothing to say in the matter; that they had requisitioned a certain number of rooms from the French authorities, and that they must go where those authorities sent them, and had no right to go elsewhere; that it was then too late to make any change that day, but that if Mr. Washburne would find them quarters elsewhere, they would cheerfully vacate all American apartments the next day. In the mean time Washburne had been to Jules Favre. Favre told him that there was every prospect that the terms of peace would be accepted by the Assembly at Bordeaux that evening, and that the Germans, in accordance with the treaty, would leave Paris the next day. They were accepted that evening; but Bismarck wished to give as many German troops as possible an opportunity to enter Paris, and so refused to accept the telegraphic announcement of the acceptance of the treaty by the Assembly. The next day the written official notice arrived, and the day after Paris was evacuated. The Germans remained in Paris three days. They did no harm. I heard of nothing missing but a few blankets. By the terms of the treaty thirty thousand were to occupy Paris. It was rumored that the garrison was changed every night, and that ninety thousand entered in all.

The attitude of the people of Paris toward the conquerors was, upon the whole, excellent. They staid away from the occupied quarter, and minded their own business. In this quarter the shops were all closed, except a few restaurants and cafés that the Germans insisted should be opened. Some of these cafés were afterward gutted by the mob, which was rather hard on the owners, as they had been compelled to open them. But a mob is never just. Some few of the populace fraternized with the invaders, and were to be seen talking amicably with them;

and some of the rougher element attempted to create a disturbance, but were soon overawed by the great numbers and martial bearing of the conquerors. While only thirty thousand were in Paris, there can be little doubt that a hundred thousand were within a half-hour's march, ready to enter to the assistance of their comrades if needed. Indeed, I imagine that all the troops who passed in review before the Emperor at Longchamps either occupied Paris, or were bivouacked in the Bois during the three days of the occupation.

They had come in very quietly, and with military precautions against surprise. They went out with a flourish of trumpets. They had bivouacked in large numbers about the Arch, and their camp-fires lighted up the inscriptions on that magnificent monument recording the victories of French over German arms. It certainly is most creditable to the conquerors that they did the Arch no harm. Few nations would have been so magnanimous. The weather was perfect, the night mild and balmy, the moon nearly full, and the beautiful German camp-songs, admirably sung, resounded in the stillness of the hour till ten o'clock struck, when perfect silence reigned in the camp. When the Germans entered Paris, they marched round the Arch; when they went out they took down the chains which inclose it, and every regiment of infantry and cavalry, and every battery of artillery passed directly under it, drums beating, colors flying, and the men cheering as they passed. They were gloriously repaid for the trials of the campaign.

Ten days passed after the surrender, and apparently the French authorities had made no provision to revictual Paris. There was no beef, to speak of, in the city, and very little mutton. The bread remained the same wretched dark stuff, one-third flour, two-thirds pease, beans, oats, rice, straw—in fact, any refuse. Delicious white bread, fresh butter, and eggs were to be bought of thé German soldiers just beyond the barriers; and any one who took the trouble, and had the means, could procure these luxuries at reasonable prices. The peasants sold them to the German soldiers, and they were permitted to resell them at a small profit. The first train of provisions to enter Paris was sent by the citizens of London, to their credit be it spoken. Will it be believed that considerable difficulty was experienced in finding persons willing to take the trouble to distribute this food gratuitously? It was done to a very limited extent at the *mairies*. The great dry-goods establishment of the Bon Marché distributed a portion; but much was stored in the Halles de l'Abondance for want of distribution, and burned up when that establishment was destroyed during the Commune. I remember hearing a Chauvin of the Assembly at Versailles pitch into the English for coming over after the Commune to visit Paris in her desolation. He was answered by Jules Favre, as happily as truly, that "the English, before they organized their trains of pleasure, had organized their trains of relief."

In this connection let me state that more than two millions of dollars were sent from the United States. At least two cargoes of provisions arrived at Havre, our Government supplying the vessels. No one could be found to distribute the supplies. The French are so government-ridden that they are unable to take the initiative in any thing for themselves. I have seen a strong, bold man, a guide in the Pyrenees, stand wringing his hands and crying, while his house was on fire, waiting for the soldiers to come and save his furniture and put out the flames. One of the shiploads of provisions I speak of was sent to London, sold there, and the proceeds distributed to the poor of France. Part of the relief sent was distributed through the Government, but experience showed this method to be slow—there was too much red-tape about it. The funds were finally placed in the hands of American ladies and gentlemen residing at Paris and Versailles, whose knowledge of France and acquaintance with French people gave them the means of making a judicious distribution. A part was expended by a committee of ladies, of which Madame MacMahon was the President; something was placed at the disposal of the Countess of Paris, out of regard for her husband, who had served in our army during the war; and a very large portion was distributed through the Sisters of Charity. Nothing could be more judicious, and at the same time more thoroughly business-like, than the manner in which these admirable women disposed of the money intrusted to them, rendering a voucher for every franc they expended. One felt that every penny in their hands had been placed where it was most needed, and would do most good.

Mr. Washburne left Paris early in February for Brussels, where his family were residing, and where, by-the-way, a very large number of our Parisian Americans had taken refuge. But he came back in a week, feeling quite poorly. He had been so overrun with visitors making inquiries or asking favors, that he had had no rest, and so returned to the lately beleaguered city for a little quiet. I remained until the Germans had made their triumphal entry, and their more triumphal departure, and then got leave and went to London to join my family.

CHAPTER XX.

The Commune.—Murder of French Generals.—The National Guard of Order.—It disbands.—The Reasons.—Flight of the Government to Versailles.—Thiers.—Attempts to reorganize National Guard.—An American arrested by Commune.—Legation intervenes.—His Discharge.—His Treatment.—Reign of King Mob.—"*Démonstrations Pacifiques.*"—Absurd Decrees of the Commune.—Destruction of the Vendôme Column.

But it has rarely been my lot, in the course of my official life, to enjoy an uninterrupted leave of absence. The present was no exception. I was scarcely fairly installed in England, and fighting "my battles o'er again," and showing "how fields were" lost, when there came a telegram from Mr. Washburne telling me that there were disturbances in Paris, and that I must return immediately. Some of the National Guard of the Belleville and Montmartre quarters had taken advantage of the confusion reigning immediately after the surrender, and seized several field-guns and mitrailleuses, and carried them off to their fastnesses on Montmartre. They now refused to surrender them; and when the Government attempted to take them, the troops fraternized with the mob, and deserted their generals, Lecompte and Thomas, whom the Communists forthwith shot. It was said that Count Bismarck had urged the disarming of the National Guard at the time of the surrender. Trochu's Government had refused. They must have bitterly regretted it afterward.

On my return I entered Paris by the Gare St. Lazare. That usually peaceful temple of traffic was thronged by *Gardes Nationaux*—" The National Guard of Order," they called themselves, or were called, to distinguish them from the Communists. These gentlemen appeared to be enjoying themselves. They were comfortably housed in the building, and lounged and chatted there, not without frequent visits to the neighboring cafés. I found that they held the Grand Hotel, and the new Opera-house, both strong positions, and within easy supporting distance of each other. They also held the Bourse, the Bank of France, the "Finances," and many other " coignes of vantage." But " coignes of vantage " are of very little use when the heart to defend them is lacking. In a very few days these men, outnumbering the Communists two or three to one, backed by the power of the Government and the wealth of Paris, and by the moral support of the Germans and of the civilized world, had disbanded, taken refuge in flight, and left their families, and their property, and their beautiful city to the tender mercies of the mob.

It was a matter of the utmost astonishment to me, and to every one with whom I conversed, that the National Guard of Order should have behaved as they did. I never understood it till I talked with my barber just after his battalion had disbanded, and before he had escaped to London. They got tired of sleeping away from their families, getting their meals irregularly, and having to pay restaurant-prices for them. They were in a state of disgust, too, with the Government, who refused to pass an act to relieve them from their rents accrued during the siege. My barber was an excellent representative of his class, the *petite bourgeoisie;* a well-to-do man, employing two apprentices, making a good livelihood, and laying by something for a *dot* for his children—economical, intelligent, sober. He belonged to the most respectable battalion in the city, that of the quarter of the "Finances." I expressed my surprise at their disbanding. He said that the Government would do nothing for them, so they would do nothing for the Government: it might put down the *émeute* itself. So they abandoned their property and their homes and their idolized Paris, shut up their shops, and ran away.

The relations between the Government and the governed in France are difficult for an American to understand. In the United States and in England the Government is *our* government, its interests are *our* interests, and we stand by and defend it, not only because it is our duty to do so, but because it is *ours*. This feeling does not exist in France among the masses, the *petit commerce* and the peasantry. They look upon the Government as a foreign body which has somehow or other—it matters very little how—got possession of power. As long as it preserves order, prevents crime, insures prosperity, and gratifies vanity by foreign conquests, it is firmly seated; but the moment it ceases to be able to do all this, let it go, and try another.

It is a strange notion of the duties of a Government that it must insure prosperity; but it prevails very generally among the masses in France, and is not unknown among the uneducated classes in other countries. The theory of the Long Island fisherman is more generally acted upon than is acknowledged: "He knew Governor Dix, and he liked Governor Dix, but he hadn't averaged an eel to a pot all summer; and he thought he would try a new governor."

The conduct of the Government, or, rather, that of M. Thiers—for at that time Thiers was the Government, and he might have said with perfect truth, "*L'état c'est moi*"—has been much and harshly criticised. Whether this criticism is just or not, depends upon the loyalty or disloyalty of the troops. If they were true to their colors and ready to fight the mob, as they afterward did, there never was a more cowardly and disgraceful surrender than the retreat to Versailles, as unwise and unmilitary as it was cowardly, for it discouraged the respectable citizens, and abandoned to the mob all the advantages of position, immense war material, and the unbounded wealth of the capital. It was proceeding upon Artemus Ward's military plan. Artemus said that if he were in a city with fifty thousand men, besieged by an enemy with fifty thousand men, he would open the gates and march out, and let them march in, and then besiege them. Artemus and M. Thiers appear to have studied in the same military school. But if, as Thiers alleged, the army could not be relied upon, but were ready to raise the butts of their muskets "*en air*" and fraternize with the Communists, then there never was a wiser movement: it was truly a "masterly retreat." Had what Thiers apprehended happened, had the troops fraternized with the mob, a movement which was only an insurrection—a bloody one, it is true, but confined to one city—would have spread over France, and there would have been a repetition, with aggravation, of all the horrors of the first Revolution.

Before the National Guard of Order disbanded, several well-intentioned efforts were made by officers of rank to effect an organization among the citizens against the insurgents. Admiral de Saissy either volunteered, or was sent by the Government, to take command. He made his head-quarters at the Grand Hôtel, within a stone's-throw of the Communists intrenched in the Place Vendôme. Here they were isolated, far from their supports at Belleville and Montmartre. Why the Admiral did not place a battery in position in the Tuileries Gardens, commanding the Place Vendôme by the Rue Castiglione, or why he did not simply starve the Communists out, I never knew: probably he could not depend upon his men. I am confirmed in this belief by a circumstance which happened within my own observation. Two or three French gentlemen called at the Legation one morning, to say that a young American friend, a Mr. Delpit, of New Orleans, had been arrested by the Communists, and was then a prisoner in the Place Vendôme, and would probably be dragged that day before a Communist court-martial, condemned, and shot. Mr. Washburne was at Versailles. I immediately sent his private secretary, an attaché of the Legation, furnished with all the necessary documents, to his relief. In a very short time Mr. M'Kean returned, after a most successful mission. He had seen Delpit, he had seen the insurgent authorities, and they had promised to discharge their prisoner that very day. They did so. The next day he came up to thank us for our prompt intervention in his behalf, which had undoubtedly saved his life. I naturally asked him how he happened to be arrested. He said that he had gone to see Admiral de Saissy, whom he knew, at the Grand Hôtel; that the Admiral was very anxious to send a dispatch to a distant part of the city; that the Admiral's aid was ready to start, but that there appeared to be a very unanimous indisposition on the part of the officers of the National Guard to accompany him; that thereupon he volunteered. The Admiral jumped at the offer, and said, "*You* will go, I know; *you* are an American; *you* are not afraid." A French commander must have been very much provoked by the conduct of the officers about him to use such language in their presence. Delpit and the aid started, but had gone but a little way, when they were surrounded by a squad of the insurgents, who ordered them to halt. Delpit drew his revolver, and threatened to shoot, while he told his companion to run. The aid escaped. The insurgents leveled their pieces, and were about to fire, when Delpit, seeing that his companion had escaped, concluded that discretion was the better part of valor, and surrendered. They disarmed him, treating him very roughly, and one of them—a negro—spat in his face. They shut him up in a cellar in the Place Vendôme, and it was likely to go hard with him, when M'Kean appeared upon the scene. Delpit told me that when they found that he was cared for by the Legation, their conduct changed marvelously. They treated him with the greatest respect, and the colored brother who had spit in his face was particularly marked in his attentions. Delpit has since distinguished himself as a poet. His work on the siege of Paris was crowned by the Academy, and he is the author of a successful play, which means much in France.

But Admiral de Saissy had had enough of it. He gave it up, and went back to Versailles. The National Guard of Order disbanded, and King Mob reigned triumphant.

At first King Mob was a good-natured monarch. He collected a lot of pitch-pine torches, and lighted them on top of the Vendôme Column. The effect was good. He made bonfires, fired off guns, organized processions, made speeches; in fact, behaved like any first-class American city on the Fourth of July. This did not last long, however. The tiger soon showed his claws. The party of order, having given up their arms and disbanded, proceeded to organize what they called a "*démonstration pacifique*," designed to produce a moral effect upon a horde of savages. They paraded the streets in large numbers unarmed. The first day's procession was rather a success. It was a novelty, and took. The second day's was not so successful. They marched up the Rue de la Paix, intending, in the grandeur of their moral strength, to pass straight through the Place Vendôme, the tiger's lair. The barricades were to disappear at their approach, the insurgents were to throw themselves into their arms, and there was to be one huge kiss of peace and reconciliation. Unfortunately, things did not turn out as set down in the bills. The barriers did not melt away, and the insurgents refused to kiss and make friends. On the contrary, they opened fire on the procession, and several of its numbers were killed. It was a well-meant effort, but Quixotic to the last degree.

And now the tiger had tasted blood, and his appetite grew by what it fed on. But his rage increased by degrees, advancing from one atrocity to another, till it culminated in the slaughter of the hostages.

There was a mixture of the ridiculous with the infamous in the early acts of the Commune. Its members were very numerous; so, for working purposes they appointed a "Committee of Public Safety," which very soon belied its name. These men appointed the ministers. To call a man "Minister of War" was not democratic, so they called him "*citoyen délégué au Ministère de la Guerre.*" The title of "General" they found inconsistent with the simplicity of republican institutions, and so suppressed it. "Colonel" could pass muster, but "General" was too aristocratic for their dainty ears. Then they found that, like other mere mortals, they must live and provide for their families. It was so much easier to pillage a shop than to work! The shop-keeper should be proud to contribute to the well-being of the brave defenders of the Republic! Then they published a decree seizing all the workshops, that they might be occupied by Communist workmen on the co-operative system. A jury was to be appointed—by the Commune, of course—to assess the value of the property, and compensation was to be made to the owner. As a practical measure, this was not a success. The workmen found it pleasanter to play soldier, and to take what they wanted, than to work even on the co-operative system. So the workshops generally remained in the hands of their owners. Next they commenced the work of demolition, and almost equaled the great Haussmann in this respect. They pulled down the house of M. Thiers (the Assembly has since built him a better one); and they passed decrees to tear down the houses of Jules Favre and other members of the Government, and confiscate their property. Happily the patriots to whom the execution of these decrees was intrusted were not perfectly immaculate; they could generally *be seen*. In this way much less irreparable injury was done than might have been expected.

One of their follies was the destruction of the Colonne Vendôme. An eminent artist—Courbet—who was a member of the Commune, said that it offended his artistic taste. Others of this band of brothers said that it perpetuated the victory of war over peace; that it kept alive a feeling of triumph in the conquerors and revenge in the conquered; that the peoples should be brothers, etc., etc. So they pulled it down; and the present Government forthwith rebuilt it, and the courts have condemned M. Courbet to pay the expense.

When the Column was pulled down, all the shop-windows within half a mile were pasted over with strips of paper to prevent their being broken by the shock. It fell, and people two hundred yards off did not know that any thing unusual had happened. It was a question much discussed how far the prostrate Column would reach. Its length was generally much overestimated. It was thought that it would extend at least one hundred feet into the Rue de la Paris. It did not enter the street, nor even cross the Place Vendôme. The bronze plates were nearly all saved. Some few were disposed of by the Communist soldiers. One was sold by a sailor to a lady for five hundred francs. He afterward denounced her to the Government, and got five hundred francs more for doing so. A profitable transaction! One was sold to an American, and made the voyage to New York, where it was found by the French Consul, reclaimed, and returned to Paris.

CHAPTER XXI.

Diplomatic Corps moves to Versailles. — Journey there and back.—Life at Versailles.—German Princes.—Battle at Clamart.—Unburied Insurgents.—Bitterness of Class Hatred.—Its Probable Causes.—United States Post-office at Versailles.—The Archbishop of Paris. — Attempts to save his Life. — Washburne's Kindness to him.—Blanqui.—Archbishop murdered.—Ultramontanism.—Bombardment by Government.—My Apartment struck.—Capricious Effects of Shells.—Injury to Arch of Triumph.—Bass-reliefs of Peace and War.

As soon as the Government had moved to Versailles, the diplomatic corps followed. Mr. Washburne hired a large room in the Rue de Mademoiselle (the sister of Louis XIV.— all Versailles bears the impress of the reign of that monarch). This room had to do for office, bedroom, and sitting-room; for Versailles was crowded, and we were lucky to get any thing so comfortable. As we had far more to do at Paris than at Versailles, and Paris was then, as always, the seat of attraction, Mr. Washburne spent four days of the week in that city, and three at Versailles, and I alternated with him. We had passes from both sides. I made the trip twice a week, and sometimes under considerable difficulties. I have traveled more than thirty miles to reach Paris from Versailles, a distance of nine miles, partly in a diligence, partly on foot, partly in flat-boats to cross the Seine where the French had most unnecessarily blown up their own beautiful bridges, and partly by rail. I suppose that I am better acquainted with the westerly environs of Paris than any foreigner but a medical student. Some of the drives in the months of April and May, especially one by Sceaux and Fontaine-les-Roses, and up the valley of the Bièvre, are very lovely.

But after a while we had a regular organized line by St. Denis. The Germans occupied this town, and insisted upon keeping open the railroad into Paris, the Chemin de Fer du Nord. They said that under the treaty they had a right to draw certain supplies from France, and that Paris was the most convenient place to draw them from, and from Paris they meant to draw them; and that if the Communists did not keep the Porte St. Denis open, *they* would. The Commune always had a wholesome fear of the Germans; this was all that restrained them from even greater outrages than they perpetrated; and they hated the Germans less than they did their own countrymen at Versailles. In going to Versailles we took the train to St. Denis; there we hired a carriage, or took the public conveyance, and so drove to our destination, a trip of about three hours in all: or we drove out by the Porte St. Denis, and so all the way to Versailles. This was generally my route, for a number of American and French friends asked me to bring their horses and carriages from the ill-fated city. If the Communist officers at the gates were close observers, they must have thought that I was the owner of one of the largest and best-appointed stables in Paris.

There was very little to do at Versailles, and perhaps less to eat. The Government was there, and the Assembly, and the Corps Diplomatique, and consequently the crowd of people who had business with these bodies, thronged to that city. At the restaurants it was a struggle to get any thing; and when you got it, it was not precisely in the Café Anglais style. I found two or three pleasant American families who had wintered here very quietly during the German occupation. They had had no occasion to complain of their treatment. At the Hôtel de France I found Dr. Hosmer, the intelligent and cultivated principal correspondent of the *Her-*

ald. That enterprising journal had its staff of couriers, who were always at our service during those days of irregular postal communication. At the Hôtel des Reservoirs several German princes, officers of the army, were lodged—intelligent, agreeable, cultivated gentlemen. They were only too glad to have the pleasure of the society of American ladies, for of course they could not visit the French; and no class of men long for and appreciate ladies' society like educated officers on campaign in an enemy's country. They eagerly accepted invitations to dine with my friends for a double reason, the pleasure of their society, and that of a good dinner; for the French cook never could manage, though of course he did his best, to cook a good dinner for the Germans, and the landlord was always just out of that favorite brand of Champagne.

The day after my first arrival at Versailles I made an excursion to the battle-field at Clamart, near Meudon. The Communists had been defeated there the day before. I had "assisted" at the battle from the Paris side. In attempting to reach Versailles in that direction, I found myself in the midst of the insurgents, and under the fire of the troops. The manner in which the insurgents behaved had not given me a very exalted idea of their soldierly qualities. It was all confusion, talking, drinking, and panic. A mob of them surged up to the gate, and demanded admission. It was refused, and they were ordered back to their regiments. But the crowd increased, and became more clamorous. The principles of fraternity forbade the guard to keep their brethren out in the cold, where the naughty Versaillais might pounce upon them; so the draw-bridge fell, the gates opened, and the runaways entered.

When I visited the battle-field, many of the dead still lay unburied, while the soldiers lounged about with their hands in those everlasting pockets, and looking with the most perfect indifference upon their dead countrymen. The class hatred which exists in France is something we have no idea of, and I trust that we never shall. It is bitter, relentless, and cruel; and is, no doubt, a sad legacy of the bloody Revolution of 1789, and of the centuries of oppression which preceded it. At the beginning of the war the peasants in one of the villages not far from Paris thrust a young nobleman into a ditch, and there burned him to death with the stubble from the fields. They had nothing particular against him, except that he was a nobleman. In Paris the mob threw the gendarmes, when they caught them, into the Seine, and when they attempted to struggle out upon the banks hacked off their hands. On the battle-field I have referred to, the *frères chrétiens*, a most devoted and excellent body of men, were moving about on their errands of mercy. Seeing these unburied bodies, they went to the commanding officer, and begged him to detail a party to bury them. He did it to oblige them. As the soldiers lifted one of the dead, a young American who accompanied me said, "Why, he hasn't a bad face after all!" At once the soldiers looked at him with suspicion, the officer asked him who he was, and, upon being told, advised him not to express any such sentiments again.

Our principal occupation at Versailles was keeping a post-office for Americans in Paris. M. Rampont, the *directeur des postes*, had escaped, with all his staff, and established the office at Versailles. The archives of the bureau of the Avenue Joséphine were placed in our Legation. The Communists were angry enough to find themselves cut off from all postal communication with the departments. It diminished their chances of success. The only means Americans had of communicating with their friends in Paris was to send their letters to the care of the

Legation at Versailles. We have received as many as fifty in one day. Two or three times a week we took or sent them to Paris. They were there mailed by the Legation, and distributed by the rebel post-office. It cost Uncle Samuel a penny or two, but he and his representatives at Washington did not grumble.

The only episode of interest that occurred at Versailles was our attempt to save the life of the Archbishop of Paris. He had been arrested by the Commune, and held as a hostage for the release of some of their own rag, tag, and bobtail. One day the Pope's Nuncio called to see Mr. Washburne. He was in Paris. The Nonce thereupon explained his business to me, and afterward sent two canons of the Metropolitan Church to see me. They came to beg Mr. Washburne to do all in his power to save the life of the Archbishop, which they considered to be in imminent danger. They had already tried one or more European embassies, but were met with the answer that they could have nothing to do with the Commune. They handed me their papers, and I went at once to Paris. Mr. Washburne took up the matter with his accustomed energy and kindliness. He got permission to see the prisoner. He took him books and newspapers and old wine. He did all in his power to negotiate an exchange with Blanqui, a veteran agitator held by the Government. The Commune consented, but the Versailles authorities would not. M. Thiers consulted his ministers and his council of deputies. They were unanimously of opinion that they could hold no dealings with the Commune. It was then proposed to let Blanqui escape, and that thereupon the Archbishop should escape too, and that there need be no negotiations whatever. This M. Thiers declined.

Matters were complicated by the conduct of the Vicar-general Lagarde. He had been a prisoner with the Archbishop, and had been released for the purpose of bringing letters to Versailles with a view to negotiate the proposed exchange, and on condition that he should return. Once safely at Versailles, he declined to go back. His pretext was that M. Thiers's letter in reply to the Archbishop's was sealed, and that he could not carry back a sealed letter in reply to one unsealed. I remember the sad and resigned, but not bitter tone, in which the Archbishop wrote of this desertion, and the exceedingly cautious terms in which the Pope's Nuncio referred to it.

But Mr. Washburne's untiring efforts were in vain. He had to contend with the *vis inertia* of French bureaucracy, and he who can move this mass must be ten times a Hercules.

The Archbishop was murdered; but Blanqui, whom the French Government held with so relentless a grip, was condemned to a year or two's imprisonment only.

I thought at that time, and think still, that no determined effort was made to save the Archbishop's life, except by two or three canons of his Church, and by the Minister of the United States. The French authorities certainly were lukewarm in the matter. The Archbishop was a Gallican, a liberal Catholic, notably so. Had he been an Ultramontane, I think that the extreme Right of the Assembly—the Legitimists—would have so exerted themselves that his life would have been saved. M. Thiers occupied a difficult position. He was suspected by the Legitimists of coquetting with the radicals, and of having no serious intention of putting down the insurrection. The suspicion was, of course, unfounded; but it may have prevented him from entering upon those informal negotiations which would probably have resulted in the release of the prisoner.

I once expressed these views to a lady in Paris, herself a liberal Catholic. She would not admit them to be true. Some weeks later, I met her again, and she told me that she believed that I was right; that she had heard such sentiments expressed by Legitimist ladies, that she was satisfied that there was an influential, if not a large, class of Ultramontanes, to whom the death of the Archbishop was not unwelcome. He has been succeeded by a noted Ultramontane.

Meantime the army was being rapidly reorganized. The Imperial Guard, and other *corps d'élite*, had returned from Germany, where they had been prisoners of war. Marshal MacMahon took command. Why M. Thiers did not then assault the city, and carry it, as he undoubtedly could have done, was a matter of surprise to every one, and especially to those whose lives and property lay at the mercies of the Commune. But Thiers had built the fortifications of Paris. He looked upon them with a paternal eye. To him they were not like other men's fortifications. They were impregnable to ordinary assault, and could only be taken by regular approaches. How I wished that Guizot had built them! We might have been saved a month of danger, loss, and intense anxiety.

On my weekly visit to Paris I had a better opportunity to observe the progress of events than if I had staid there without interruption, while my residence of three days gave me ample occasion to appreciate the full pleasures of the bombardment. It must always be a mystery why the French bombarded so persistently the quarter of the Arch of Triumph—the West End of Paris—the quarter where nine out of ten of the inhabitants were known friends of the Government. They had their regular hours for this *divertissement*, for so they seemed to regard it. They took a turn at it before breakfast, to give them an appetite; and at five o'clock in the morning I was waked by the shells from Mont Valérien bursting and crashing in the Place de l'Etoile. About noon they went at it again, and when I went home to breakfast (*anglice* lunch), I had to dodge round corners, and take refuge behind stone columns. Then, just before sunset, they always favored us with an evening gun, for good-night. The days, too, were so confoundedly long at that season of the year—April and May—and the weather provokingly fine. How I longed for a delicious London fog!

I remember one day, as I dodged behind a stone

pillar in the Rue de Presbourg to avoid a coming shell, the *concierge* called me in. I went into his *loge*, but declined to go into the cellar, where his wife and children had taken refuge. He had two *loges*, and I strongly advised him to move into the unoccupied one as the safer of the two, for I had observed that the shells generally passed easily enough through one stone wall, but were arrested by a second. He took my advice. The next day a shell from one of their evening guns fell into the window of the *loge* he had left, passed through the floor into the cellar, and there exploded, and tore every thing to pieces.

My own apartment was struck eight times by fragments of shells. Fortunately but one exploded in the house, and that two stories above me. It shattered the room into which it fell fearfully, but, strange to say, did no damage in the adjoining rooms. Happily the apartment was unoccupied. The tenants, a few days before, had taken advantage of a law of the Commune which released all tenants from their rent if they found it inconvenient to pay it, and had decamped, furniture and all.

Mr. Washburne advised me to change my residence, as it was not safe. But I felt that the dignity of the great American people would not permit even one of its subordinate representatives to leave the building while a Frenchman remained in it. Mr. Washburne's practice, too, was not in accordance with his precepts. If we heard of any part of Paris where shells were likely to burst and bullets to whistle, Washburne was sure to have important business in that direction.

I was not in my house when the shell exploded. I generally came home to dinner after dark. If there is any thing thoroughly disagreeable, it is to have shells tumbling and bursting about you when you are at dinner. It is bad enough at breakfast, but the dinner-hour should be sacred from vulgar intrusion.

I recollect one day after my midday breakfast, as I left my house, I saw a knot of men standing on the corner of the Avenue de l'Impératrice and the Rue de Presbourg; I thought that I would go and see what was up. Mont Valérien was blazing away at a great rate. As I joined the group, one of them said, "They'll fire at us soon, seeing half a dozen people here." He had hardly said so, when there was a flash, and a puff of smoke, and in a minute we heard the huge shell hurtling through the air. It missed us, of course, and fell in the Place, and exploded. All these men were friends of the Government, and they were looking to Mont Valérien for help, longing for the troops to come in. This was the protection the Government gave its friends, "the protection which the vulture gives the lamb, covering and devouring it."

About once a week I was called in by some neighboring *concierge* to note the damage done by shells in apartments belonging to Americans. Shells are strangely capricious. One end of No. 8 Rue de Presbourg, opposite my own residence, was nearly torn to pieces; the other end was untouched. At No. 12, shell after shell penetrated the kitchen departments, while the *salons* were uninjured. I was called to see the damage done to the *premier* of No. 8, a beautiful apartment belonging to a New York lady. A shell had entered the *salon* and exploded. I have never seen more thorough destruction. The mirrors were shattered; the floors and ceilings rent and gaping; sofas, chairs, and tables upset and broken. In the midst of all this destruction stood a little table with a lady's work-basket upon it, the needle in the work, the thimble and scissors on the table, as if she had left them five minutes before —the only objects unhurt in the room. It was a touching souvenir of peaceful domestic life in the midst of the worst ravages of war.

Mr. Washburne and Lord Lyons complained to Jules Favre of this persistent bombardment, for the property destroyed and the lives endangered were largely American and English. He replied that it was "bad shooting," but he smiled as he said so, and evidently did not believe it himself. It was sheer wantonness, that irrepressible desire of artillery-men, of which I have before spoken, to hit something—an enemy if possible, a friend if no enemy offers.

It was singular that while so many shells fell in the immediate neighborhood of the Arch of Triumph, so little serious injury was done to it. I remarked a curious circumstance in this connection. The bass-reliefs on the arch facing the Avenue de la Grande Armée are Peace and War—on the right, as you face the Arch, War; on the left, Peace. War was very much injured; Peace was scarcely touched.

CHAPTER XXII.

Reign of Terror.—Family Quarrels.—The Alsacians, etc., claim German Nationality.—They leave Paris on our Passes.—Prisoners of Commune.—Priests and Nuns.—Fragments of Shells.—"Articles de Paris."—Fearful Bombardment of "Point du Jour."—Arrest of Cluseret.—Commune Proclamations.—Capture of Paris.—Troops enter by Undefended Gate.—Their Slow Advance.—Fight at the Tuileries Gardens.—Communist Women.—Capture of Barricades.—Cruelties of the Troops.—"Pétroleuses."—Absurd Stories about them.—Public Buildings fired.—Destruction of Tuileries, etc., etc. —Narrow Escape of Louvre.—Treatment of Communist Prisoners. —Presents from Emperor of Germany.

As time passed, the puerilities and atrocities of the Commune kept equal pace. They had taken possession of the public buildings and raised the red flag upon them, suppressing the tricolor. They now passed a decree requiring every man to be provided with a *carte d'identité;* this, they said, was to protect them against Government spies. They established a bureau of denunciation, where any man who had a grudge against his neighbor had simply to denounce him as a Versailles sympathizer, and he was arrested. They closed the churches, or turned them into clubs. They arrested the priests; they shut up some of the convents, and imprisoned the nuns. They confiscated the gold and silver church plate, and turned it into coin. It was emphatically a "Reign of Terror." It was estimated that within a month after the outbreak of the Commune three hundred thousand people left Paris.

In the clubs they denounced the Legation. They said that Mr. Washburne was about to call in the Germans at the request of the diplomatic corps. They proposed to hang him, and to banish the rest of us. In point of fact, I believe that Mr. Washburne could have called in the German army at any time. He had only to report to General Manteuffel that the lives of the Germans in Paris were in danger, and that he found himself unable to protect them, and Manteuffel would have occupied Paris at once. But Mr. Washburne never entertained an idea of doing this.

Then the Commune began to quarrel among themselves. The Happy Family was at variance. Strange as it may appear, at the beginning of the affair, there were many earnest, honest fanatics in Paris who joined the movement. The first demands of the Commune under the influence of these men were not unreasonable, in American eyes. They asked that they might elect their own prefect, and that Paris should not be garrisoned by Government soldiers. But events soon outstripped these men; and as they found the city given over to organized pillage—the Committee of Public Safety meeting in secret, instead of in the light of open day, as they had promised, and the model republic of which they had dreamed as much a chimera as ever—they withdrew from the Government. Over twenty of them withdrew in a body, and published their reasons for doing so. But the scoundrels who now directed the movement "cared for none of these things." They had used these poor enthusiasts while it suited their purpose; now they threw them overboard, and replied to their manifesto by removing the Committee of Public Safety as too mild, afflicted with scruples, and appointing one of a bloodier type, one of its members a murderer.

During all this time the Legation was beset from morning till night. The Alsacians and Lorrains residing in Paris, whom the treaty had made Germans, but who were nevertheless permitted to choose their nationality, had fully intended to *opter* for the French, and refused with indignation a German nationality. But when they found that to remain French condemned them to the National Guard, while to become German enabled them to leave Paris, and return to their homes, they came in shoals to the Legation to ask for German passports. It was a renewal of the days before the siege, the days of the German expulsion. Much of Mr. Washburne's time was taken up in visiting German prisoners, and procuring their discharge, and sometimes that of French priests and nuns. To procure the release of Germans was no very difficult task, for the Commune, as I have said, had a wholesome fear of the Teuton, and *"Civis Germanicus sum"* was an open-sesame to Communist prison-doors. But to release the poor French nuns was a more difficult task. Mr. Washburne effected it in many instances; but it required all his energy and decision.

And here I must remark how much better and more humane it was to do as Mr. Washburne did—to hold such communication with the officials of the Commune as was absolutely necessary, and so save human life, and mitigate human suffering—than to sit with folded arms, and say, "Really, I can have nothing to do with those people," and so let fellow-creatures suffer and perish.

Where there is a will, there is generally a way. Mr. Washburne was able to assist and protect indirectly many persons whom he could not claim as American citizens or German subjects. We could not give a United States passport to a Frenchman, but we could make him a bearer of dispatches, give him a courier's pass, and so get him safely out of Paris. Colonel Bonaparte escaped in this way. He was on the "Black List" of the Commune for arrest, and arrest then meant death.

As the siege progressed, the bombardment became more and more severe. The beautiful avenue of the Champs Elysées was like a city of the dead. Not a living creature was to be seen upon it for hours. From time to time a man would emerge cautiously from a side street, gaze anxiously up the avenue, then start on a run to cross it. But the "insatiate thirst of gold" is stronger than the fear of death; and, at the worst of the bombardment, men and boys were to be seen lurking near the Arch, and darting upon an exploding shell to secure its fragments while they were still too hot to hold. A large business was done in these fragments after the siege, as well as in the unexploded shells. They were sold as relics; and the Parisian shop-keepers mounted them as clocks, fenders, inkstands, penholders, and other *articles de Paris*.

A battery of immense strength was at length erected at Montretout, near St. Cloud. It was probably the most powerful battery ever erected in the world. It opened upon the gate of the Point du Jour, and in a few days the scene of devastation in that quarter was fearful. Not a house was left standing, scarcely a wall. Bodies of soldiers of the National Guard lay unburied among the ruins. The fire was too hot for their comrades to approach them.

In the mean time dissension reigned among the Communists. A new Committee of Public Safety was appointed. They arrested Cluseret, their Minister of War, as they had already arrested Lullier. They accused him of treason, and it would have gone hard with him had the Commune continued much longer in power. They said that "a hideous plot had been discovered," but that the guilty were known, and "their punishment should be exemplary as their crime was unparalleled." They announced that if the Commune fell, they would fire the city, and its beauty and its pride should be buried with them. They wrote forcibly, those fellows! Had they fought with as much vigor as they wrote, the world would at least have respected their courage, instead of pronouncing them as cowardly as they were cruel. But their career of crime and folly was drawing to a close.

One day a citizen of Paris, a civil engineer, was taking his afternoon walk. As he approached one of the gates, not far from Auteuil, he was surprised to find no National Guard on duty. He kept on, and came to the fortifications. There was not a defender in sight, while the French troops lay outside under cover watching for some one to fire at. Why they had not discovered the absence of the enemy can only be accounted for by the general inefficiency into which the French army had fallen. The engineer raised his white handkerchief on his cane, and when he saw that it was observed, quietly walked through the ruins of the work, crossed the fosse, and asked the officer in command why on earth he did not come in; there was a gate, and no one to defend it. It occurred to the officer that it might be as well to do so; that perhaps that was what he was there for: so he marched in with his company, and Paris was taken. It was rather an anticlimax! After a delay of months, and a fierce bombardment, to enter Paris on the invitation of a citizen taking his afternoon walk! It was never known how that gate came to be left unguarded. It was probably owing to dissensions in the Commune. The battalion holding it had not been relieved, as they expected to be; so they voted that they would not stay any longer, shouldered their muskets, and marched off.

The troops entered on the 22d of May. Once fairly in, the work was comparatively easy; but they proceeded with great caution. It was said that Gallifet urged that he should take his cavalry, and scour the city. I believe that he could have done it on that day, for the Communists were thoroughly demoralized; but it was thought to be too hazardous an operation for cavalry. The next morning the troops advanced unopposed as far as the Place de la Concorde. I have the word of an American friend, whose apartment looked upon the Place, that the strong barricade which connected the Rue St. Florentin with the Tuileries Gardens was then undefended, and that if the troops had advanced promptly they could have carried it without resistance; but while they sent forward their skirmishers, who found no one to skirmish with, and advanced with the utmost caution, a battery, followed by a battalion of the National Guard, galloped up from the Hôtel de Ville. The troops then began regular approaches. They entered the adjoining houses, passing from roof to roof, and occupying the upper windows, till finally they commanded the barricade, and fired down upon its defenders. They filled barrels with sand, and rolled them toward the barrier. Each barrel covered two skirmishers, who alternately rolled the barrel and picked off the defenders of the barricade if they ventured to show themselves. My informant saw a young and apparently good-looking woman spring upon the barricade, a red flag in her hand, and wave it defiantly at the troops. She was instantly shot dead. When the work was carried, an old woman was led out to be shot. She was placed with her back to the wall of the Tuileries Gardens, and, as the firing party leveled their pieces, she put her fingers to her nose, and worked them after the manner of the defiant in all ages, or, as Dickens expresses it, "as if she were grinding an imaginary coffee-mill."

Many of their strongest positions were abandoned by the insurgents, having been turned by the troops. Those that resisted fell one after the other, carried in the way I have described. Indeed, I can see no possibility of a barricade holding out unless the adjacent houses are held too. That at the head of the Rue St. Florentin was of great strength, a regular work; for the Communists had several excellent engineers in their ranks, graduates of the military schools, men who had been disappointed under the Government in not meeting with the promotion they thought they deserved, and so joined the Commune. The ditch of the barricade St. Florentin was about sixteen feet deep. It made a convenient burying-ground. The dead Communists, men and women, were huddled into it, quicklime added, and the fosse filled up. As the pleasure-seeker enters the Rue de Rivoli from the Place de la Concorde he passes over the bodies of forty or fifty miserable wretches—most of them scoundrels of the deepest dye—but among them some wild fanatics, and some poor victims of the Commune, forced unwillingly into its ranks.

Much must be pardoned to soldiers heated with battle, and taught to believe every prisoner they take an incarnate devil. But making all allowances, there is no excuse for the wholesale butcheries committed by the troops. A friend of mine saw a house in the Boulevard Malesherbes visited by a squad of soldiers. They asked the *concierge* if there were any Communists concealed there. She answered that there were none. They searched the house, and found one. They took him out and shot him, and then shot her. One of the attachés of the Legation saw in the Avenue d'Autin the bodies of six children, the eldest apparently not over fourteen, shot to death as *pétroleuses*, suspected of carrying petroleum to fire the houses. There was no trial of any kind, no drum-head court-martial even, such as the laws of civilized warfare require under all circumstances. Any lieutenant ordered prisoners to be shot as the fancy took him, and no questions were asked. Many an innocent spectator perished in those days. An English officer had a narrow escape. He approached a crowd of prisoners halted for a moment on the Champs Elysées; and when they moved on, the guard roped him in with the rest, and would not listen to a word of explanation. Happily he was able to attract the attention of the Marquis de Gallifet and explain his position. An officer of high rank who was escorting a batch of prisoners to Versailles is said to have halted in the Bois, ridden down the column, picked out those whose faces he particularly disliked, and had them shot on the spot. The number of lives taken after the defeat of the Commune can never be accurately known; but it was generally computed at the time to exceed the number of those lost in both sieges.

Petroleum next became the madness of the hour. Every woman carrying a bottle was suspected of being a *pétroleuse.* The most absurd stories were told of its destructive properties. Organized bands of women were said to be patrolling the streets armed with bottles of petroleum. This they threw into the cellar windows, and then set fire to it. The windows were barred, and the cellars in Paris are universally built in stone and concrete. How they effected their purpose under these circumstances is not readily seen. If this was their *modus operandi,* they were the most inexpert incendiaries ever known. The Commune should blush for its pupils in crime. I do not believe in the petroleum story, and I do not think that one-third of the population believed in it. Yet such was the power of suspicion in those days, and such the distrust of one's neighbor, that every staid and sober housekeeper bricked up his cellar windows, and for weeks in the beautiful summer weather not an open window was to be seen on the lower stories. No doubt every second man thought it a great piece of folly thus to shut out light and air from his lower stories; but if he had not done as his neighbors did, he would have been denounced by them as a *pétroleux*.

The leaders of the Commune, as I have said, had sworn that, if the city were taken, they would blow up the public buildings, and bury every thing in a common ruin. Happily, their good-will exceeded their ability. They had no time to execute their atrocious projects. They burned the Tuileries, the Finances, the Hôtel de Ville, the Comptes, the Hotel of the Legion of Honor, and a small portion of the Palais Royal. The only irreparable loss was that of the Hôtel de Ville. The Finances, the Comptes, and the Legion of Honor had no imperishable historical associations connected with them. The Tuileries was an old and inconvenient building. The Emperor had already rebuilt it in part. Plans for reconstructing the whole building had been prepared and still exist, and nothing but the want of money had prevented their being carried into execution long before.

I do not propose to dwell upon the horrors of the nights of the 23d and 24th of May, when all Paris appeared to be in flames. The view from the high ground upon which the Legation stands was very striking. A pall of smoke hung over the city by day, and pillars of fire lighted it by night. One of the most painful features of those days was the prolonged suspense. We did not know which of the magnificent monuments of Paris were in flames; for the troops permitted no approach, and the most startling rumors were current. The Louvre was at one time in danger, but happily escaped.

I pass over, too, the cruelties of the march of the prisoners to Versailles, and the sufferings they there endured. These things are written in the annals of the times, and no good can be done by reviving them. Beautiful France has been sorely tried with revolutions. Let us hope that she has seen the last.

In the hotel of the German Embassy at Paris may be seen several articles of value, mostly Sèvres and Dresden china, which the German Government desires to present to Mr. Washburne, General Read, and some few other officers of the United States, in token of its gratitude for services rendered to German subjects during the war. These articles can not be received without the permission of Congress. The House promptly passed the joint resolution.

The Senate still hesitates. Mr. Fox, formerly Assistant Secretary of the Navy, and the officers who accompanied him to Russia, were permitted to receive such presents as "the Emperor might see fit to give them." Are Mr. Washburne and his subordinates, who certainly rendered some services, and suffered some hardships, less entitled to receive this permission than Mr. Fox and his companions, who took a monitor to Cronstadt?

THE END.

www.ingramcontent.com/pod-product-compliance
Lightning Source LLC
Chambersburg PA
CBHW032103220426
43664CB00008B/1115